ANTHROPOLOGICAL PAPERS
MUSEUM OF ANTHROPOLOGY, UNIVERSITY OF MICHIGAN
No. 79

# THE FOXIE OTTER SITE

A MULTICOMPONENT OCCUPATION NORTH OF
LAKE HURON

by
Christopher C. Hanks

Ann Arbor
1988

© 1988 by The Regents of The University of Michigan

Printed in the United States of America
All rights reserved

ISBN 0-915703-14-9

Cover design by Marty Somberg

Library of Congress Cataloging in Publication Data

Hanks, Christopher C.
  The foxie otter site : a multicomponent occupation north of Lake Huron / by Christopher C. Hanks.
  p. cm.—(Anthropological papers / Museum of Anthropology, University of Michigan ; no. 79)
  Bibliography: p.
  Appendices: 1. Fauna analysis of the foxie otter site / by Norman Haywood—2. Archaeobotanical remains from the foxie otter site / by Rodolphe Fecteau and John K. McAndrews—3. Radiocarbon date reports for the 1981 season—4. Residue analysis of stone tools and flakage and determination of site function / by Michael Broderick.
  ISBN 0-915703-14-9 (pbk.)
  1. Foxie Otter Site (Ont.) 2. Indians of North America—Ontario—Antiquities. 3. Chippewa Indians—Antiquities. 4. Excavations (Archaeology)—Ontario. 5. Ontario—Antiquities. I. Title.
II. Series: Anthropological papers (University of Michigan. Museum of Anthropology) ; no. 79.
GN2.M5 no. 79
[E78.05]
306 s—dc19
[971.3'2]                                                                88-19529
                                                                            CIP

*To Edward S. Rogers*

# Contents

| | |
|---|---|
| List of figures | vi |
| List of tables | vii |
| Acknowledgments | ix |
| CHAPTER 1. Introduction | 1 |
| CHAPTER 2. Geology and Regional Paleoenvironment | 13 |
| CHAPTER 3. History of Field Research and Methodology | 19 |
| CHAPTER 4. The Analysis of CdHk-3 | 23 |
| CHAPTER 5. Summary and Conclusions | 69 |
| References Cited | 77 |
| Appendix 1<br>Faunal Analysis of the Foxie Otter Site, by Norman Haywood | 81 |
| Appendix 2<br>Archaeobotanical Remains from the Foxie Otter Site, by<br>Rodolphe Fecteau and John H. McAndrews | 85 |
| Appendix 3<br>Sample of Data Submitted to SFU Radiocarbon Laboratory | 95 |
| Appendix 4<br>Residue Analysis of Stone Tools and Flakage and<br>Determination of Site Function, by Michael Broderick | 99 |

# Figures

| | | |
|---|---|---|
| 1. | Map of the Fox Lake area | 5 |
| 2. | McBean map of the Spanish River drainage | 8 |
| 3. | Foxie Otter site, CdHk-3 | 20 |
| 4. | Floor plan of ScE 1N0E | 30 |
| 5. | Profile of ScE 1N0E | 31 |
| 6. | Floor plan of ScE 7N0E | 32 |
| 7. | Profile of ScE 7N0E | 33 |
| 8. | Floor plan of ScE 8N0E | 34 |
| 9. | Profile of ScE 8N0E | 35 |
| 10. | Floor plan of 38°14N1W | 37 |
| 11. | Profile of 38°14N1W | 38 |
| 12. | Floor plan of 38°14N0W | 39 |
| 13. | Profile of 38°14N0W | 40 |
| 14. | Profile of south wall, 38°10N1W | 41 |
| 15. | Typing key for lithic tools | 44 |
| 16. | Typing key for lithic debitage | 46 |
| 17. | Archaic graywacke core tools | 47 |
| 18. | Archaic graywacke core tools | 48 |
| 19. | Woodland flake tools | 49 |
| 20. | Woodland flake tools | 50 |
| 21. | Woodland flake tools | 51 |

# Tables

| | | |
|---|---|---|
| 1. | Carbon-14 dates from CdHk-3 | 24 |
| 2. | Summary of tool types | 46 |
| 3. | Percentage of tool types present at CdHk-3 | 52 |
| 4. | Breakdown of tool weight for CdHk-3 | 52 |
| 5. | Anova of tool type, material and area | 53 |
| 6. | Breakdown of tools by weight and site area | 53 |
| 7. | Lithic raw material used in tools by site area | 53 |
| 8. | Tool use residue analysis | 56 |
| 9. | Residues by tool type | 56 |
| 10. | Frequency of raw material types | 64 |
| 11. | Flake type frequencies | 64 |
| 12. | Breakdown of debitage weight | 64 |
| 13. | Hypotheses for debitage tested via Cramer's $V$ | 65 |
| 14. | Cramer's $V$ test scores | 65 |

# Acknowledgments

The excavation and interpretation of the Foxie Otter site was possible due to the collaboration and assistance of many people. First, Laurie and Tutti Blake, owners of the Fox Lake Lodge. Without their support and friendship this project would never have taken place.

Claude Kerr and the INCo Department of Central Utilities supported the 1980 survey of CdHk-3 as a part of the Spanish River Archaeological Survey. In 1981, INCo again helped the research by loaning us field equipment. Materials for comparative purposes from site CdHk-3 and -14 on Fox Lake were provided by Helen Devereux and Ken Buchanan of the Archaeological Survey of Sudbury at Laurentian University.

Over the two years of research, Alex Sago, Nick Adams, Christine Adams, Nancy Hanks and Norman Haywood all worked on the site.

The analyses presented in the appendices were ably conducted by Norman Haywood, Rodolphe Fecteau, John McAndrews and Michael Broderick.

The drafting was done by Moira Irvine, Dianne Benke, Nick Adams, Kathie Stevenson and Ben Nind of Rangifer Systems.

David Pokotylo, J. V. Wright and Thor Conway offered valuable advice in conducting the analysis.

Nancy Hanks, Margaret Bertulli, Marc Stevenson and J. V. Wright read and commented on the several preliminary drafts of this manuscript.

Research on the Foxie Otter site was funded by the Ontario Heritage Foundation and INCo Metals Ltd.

Though these people all contributed to the Fox Lake Archaeological Project, the interpretation of the data is ultimately the responsibility of the author.

# 1
# INTRODUCTION

## The Foxie Otter Site and Great Lakes Prehistory

Perched on the shore of Fox Lake, 53 kilometers inland from Lake Huron, the Foxie Otter site contains one of the longest archaeological records in the upper Great Lakes (see Fig. 1). The site was used by native groups the from the interregnum period between the Early Paleo-Indian and the Early Archaic (Mason 1971:114) into the Postcontact period. Given its location slightly above the high waters of Lake Algonquin, it has been undisturbed by the rapid rise and fall of the Great Lakes in the postglacial period. Located off the classical beach ridges and not in association with a massive quarry, it offers a unique opportunity to examine the inland adaptation of the native people of the region over a 7000-year period. The excellent horizontal separation of components on the site has allowed archaeologists the chance to constructively work with the dispersed remains which are so typical of the Canadian Shield. The future of archaeology along the north side of the upper Great Lakes is tied to the development of effective methodologies for dealing with small disperse sites.

## History of the Spanish River Route

Understanding native utilization of the Foxie Otter site requires a regional perspective. Especially important to interpreting the Spanish River system is understanding the continuity of use over time, seasonal settlement shifts and the different usage patterns of the lakes and rivers.

Today, the north shore region is the home of southern Ojibwa groups who reside near Sault Ste. Marie, Thessalon, Mississagi River, Serpent River, Spanish River, Whitefish River and Whitefish Lake (Rogers 1978:764). These people are closely related to the Ottawa[1] on Manitoulin Island at Sucker Creek, Sheguiandah, West Bay, and Wikwemikong.

Most of the Ojibwa families who still use the Spanish River now live either

---

[1]This spelling is used throughout this book because it is more common in archaeological literature. "Odawa" is linguistically more correct and is the preferred spelling of the contemporary Odawa people.

at Sagamok, near the La Cloche Lake portage from the Spanish River to the old La Cloche post (south of Massey, Ontario), or around the mouth of the river at Spanish, Ontario. Other old Spanish families are now at Whitefish Lake, Sucker Creek, and West Bay.

The history of the Ojibwa and Ottawa along the north shore contains traces of the influence of the more complex tribal groups in the southern reaches Great Lakes riverine region. Unlike their more southerly neighbors, however, whose practice of maize agriculture and seasonal hunting and gathering allowed large semipermanent summer riverine villages and winter camps, north shore subsistence requires a more transient existence characterized by a band level of social organization (Callender 1978:610). Except for growing limited quantities of corn and producing maple sugar, the traditional adaptation to the north shore more closely resembled life in the boreal forest to the north than the lake forests to the south.

On many of the islands along the north shore, from the French River to the Mississagi River, small quantities of corn were grown (Rogers 1978:763). This limited horticulture was taking place prior to 1650, but its exact antiquity along the north shore is unknown (Bertulli 1981:9). Maple sugar was produced along the north shore (Rogers 1978:764; Bertulli 1981:11) and as far into the interior as Fox Lake. Sturgeon and whitefish taken in September and October, however, provided the essential stock of dried food necessary for winter survival in a land where starvation was not uncommon (Rogers 1978:762, 764).

Native life along the Spanish River in the late nineteenth and early twentieth centuries was one in which trapping provided a cash crop that supplemented fishing in the fall, hunting rabbits and partridge in the winter, and tending crops in the spring and summer (Rogers 1978:765). Gardening and large-scale fishing generally occurred near the river mouths along Lake Huron, while most trapping and hunting occurred inland. The shores of interior lakes formed the locus of settlement for the latter activities.

Traditionally, the study of native life along the north shore has been dominated by the role of the Ottawa and Ojibwa traders in the western expansion of the fur trade. By tracing the history of the local trade back in time, however, we get some glimpse of native life along the Spanish or "Sagumauc" River (Bigsby 1850:108).

After the railroad bisected the Spanish River valley in 1883, the Hudson's Bay Company opened a trading post (CfHk-3) 42 kilometers north of Fox Lake, on Kingsley Island in Pogamasing Lake (PAM, HBCA, D. 25/4, fo. 70[2]). The railroad relegated to history an old but difficult canoe route up the heavily rapided and shallow Spanish. John Sago, an elder at Sagamok, main-

---

[2]Provincial Archives of Manitoba, Hudson's Bay Company Archives.

tained that it could take a month for heavily loaded canoes to go up the river to Biscostasing Lake near the height-of-land.

The earliest map of the Spanish route was drawn by Chief Factor John McBean in 1827 (Fig. 2) (PAC,[3] HBCA, D.5/2, fo. 257). From McBean's descriptions, it is uncertain if European traders actually used the tract themselves. The notations on his map do not mention Biscostasing Lake and indicate that his knowledge of the east branch toward the height-of-land northeast of the Spanish was incomplete. Further, McBean makes no reference to Fox Lake although he does mention Gough and Pogamasing lakes. The lower Spanish route by way of the Wanapatei River, however, was used by the Hudson's Bay Company to supply Fort Temiskaming (Mitchell 1977:145–46). When the Hudson's Bay Company moved the post from La Cloche Island to the mouth of La Cloche Creek in 1821, they placed it at the head of the Spanish portage.

By the seventeenth century, the French, under Champlain, had penetrated into the upper Great Lakes. Jesuit priests established missions in Huronia (between Lake Simcoe and the Bruce Peninsula), and later on the eastern shore of Manitoulin Island near Wekwemikong (ca. 1658). According to the priests the Algonquin groups along the north shore of Lake Huron were called the Amikovek (Beaver), Archirigovans (Bass, located on the Spanish River), Nikikovek (Otter, on the Thessalon River), Mississauga (Blind River), and the Paouitagoung (Sault Ste. Marie) (Thwaites 1901:(33)149).[4] The *Jesuit Relations* of 1657–58 describes the Archirigovans controlling one of the routes by which trade to the Cree on James Bay was possible:

> The Archirigovans, who live on a river emptying into the fresh-water sea of the Hurons, go in a few days to trade with the Ataovabovskatouk Kilistinons (French for Cree), who are on the sea shore... [Thwaites 1901:(44)243]

At the time of direct contact, the Spanish route was thus recognized by the French as one of the paths to the Cree along James Bay.

Indirect contact with European goods began for native groups in the upper Great Lakes in the sixteenth century after Cartier visited the St. Lawrence. Once the European fishing industry regularly started to trade with bands along the Gulf of St. Lawrence, the quantity of goods that filtered to the interior increased. This trade may have taken place in a very roundabout manner. Evidence indicates that the St. Lawrence Iroquois and the Huron

---

[3]Public Archives of Canada.
[4]Translation of the Ojibwa band names and their locations along the north shore were determined from the editorial comments made on the *Jesuit Relations* by William Curran. He was an early twentieth-century amateur linguist from Sault Ste. Marie who spent summers traveling with the Ojibwa from the Garden River Reserve. Curran's copy of the *Relations* can be found in the Sault Ste. Marie (Ontario) Public Library.

were at war during the late Precontact and early Contact period. Because war blocked the Ottawa Valley–French River route, the Algonquins were forced to go north toward James Bay and then south again to the Saguenay and Lake St. John (Trigger 1976:197). Proto-Huron or Algonquin ceramics found at Matabachouvian on Lake St. John in Quebec suggest that either proto-Huron people or Algonquins traveled east after A.D. 1400 (Trigger 1966:171). During the sixteenth century, copper from the Lake Superior region was reaching the Saguenay River in Quebec, possibly through the hands of Nipissing rather than Huron traders (Trigger 1976:171). The Spanish route may have been one way to avoid the conflicts to the south.

From the historic record, it is obvious that the Spanish was an important trade route throughout the Postcontact period. By analogy it is assumed that this trade had its basis in the Precontact period.

## Archaeological Research in the Spanish River Drainage

Archaeological work in the Spanish River can be broken down into three broad geographic areas: (1) the lower Spanish below Agnew Lake, and the La Cloche fur trade post; (2) the Spanish from Agnew Lake to Pogamasing Lake, including the interior lakes Gough, Sinaminda, Fox, and Spanish; and (3) the headwaters of the Spanish at Biscotasing Lake (see Fig. 1). Agnew Lake is a human-made lake created by hydroelectric development at High Falls. Its shorelines are therefore not considered in this analysis.

The lower Spanish River has received the most archaeological attention. The first surveys in the area were carried out by Kalowicz and Pammett in 1968 for the Ministry of Natural Resources. They surveyed the site of the La Cloche fur trade post on the north channel of Lake Huron, east of the mouth of the Spanish River. Survey at LaCloche was continued in 1969 by Orlandine and Shaughnessy. The Royal Ontario Museum (ROM) became involved at La Cloche in 1970 when Walter Kenyon conducted test excavations at the post. A summary of research at La Cloche by Thor Conway of the Ministry of Citizenship and Culture (MCC) notes that the early work concentrated upon the historic fur trade post and overlooked the prehistoric component of the site (1977:2).

Work by the ROM continued in 1971, when Peter Storck did an archaeological survey of the town of Massey, the Spanish River Indian Reserve at Sagamok, and the La Cloche fur post. Two sites were located along the La Cloche portage and a prehistoric component was found at the post. A small lithic scatter was found on La Cloche Lake. The Reupke House site along La Cloche Creek has an historic occupation overlaying a few flakes (Storck 1971:5). On a terrace behind the La Cloche post, near the creek, a fairly extensive prehistoric concentration was discovered. Storck recovered a side-

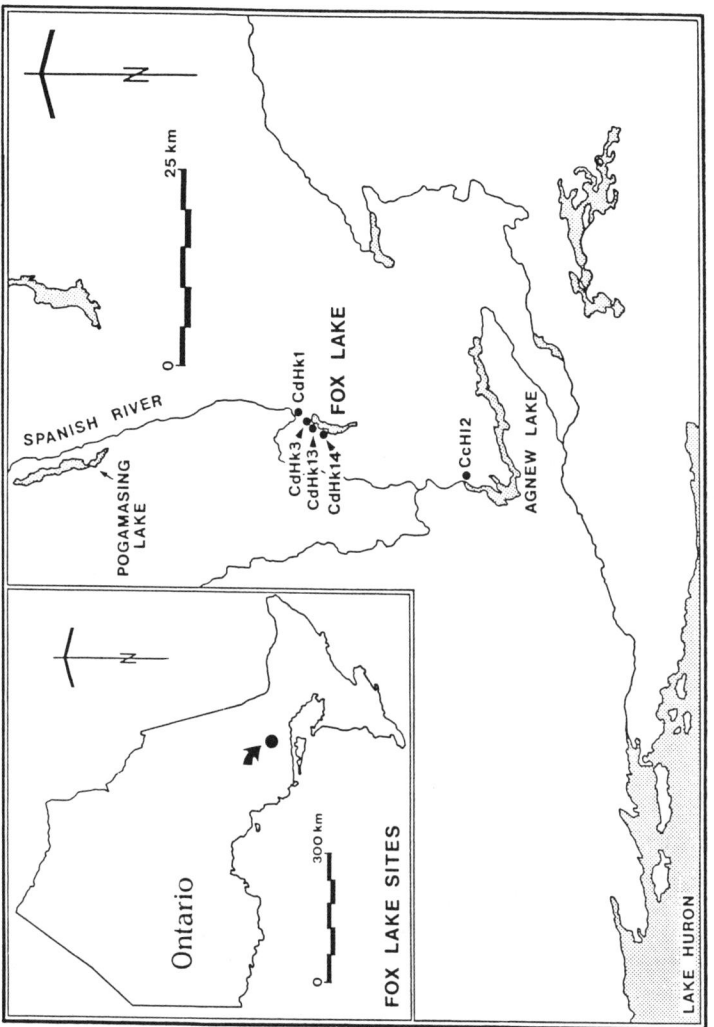

Figure 1. Map of Fox Lake area.

notched quartzite projectile point in association with grit-tempered ceramic rim and body sherds (1971:4).

Beginning in 1975, Thor Conway of the MCC started systematically examining the La Cloche site. Excavation of historic remains at the La Cloche post has identified six stratigraphic layers of fur trade remains belonging to various Northwest and Hudson's Bay Company occupations between 1759 and 1900 (Conway 1977:2).

Conway tentively indentified Storck's grit-tempered pottery as a Middle Woodland pseudo-scallopshell form from around A.D. 300. Evidence from the Mississagi delta, in the next major drainage to the west, and the Fox Lake sequence suggest that further research along the lower Spanish should reveal a Late Woodland occupation from circa 1200 B.P through the Terminal Woodland and Early Contact period, about 1650 (Bertulli 1981:286).

The Salter site (CbHm-2) is located near the confluence of the Spanish and Aux Sables River. It contained both lithic remains and grit-tempered pottery (Storck 1971:2). Thor Conway has typologically dated a small Archaic site located on a terrace overlooking the Aux Sables River, a short distance from its junction with the Spanish River. According to Conway, a vein quartz side notch point from the Hobbs site is very similar to Late Archaic material from the Marks Bay sequence along the St. Mary's River in Sault Ste. Marie (for references see Conway 1980). The most remarkable feature about the collection from this site is the tremendous size of the chipped siltstone celts. The largest is 40 cm long and 5 cm wide. Unfortunately, the remains of this site are now under a golf course.

The archaeology of the lower section of the river demonstrates both Precontact and Postcontact use of the portage route from Lake Huron to the Spanish River, via La Cloche Creek and La Cloche Lake. Though several of the lithic components are not diagnostic of any particular Precontact period, the Middle Woodland ceramics from La Cloche post and the Late Archaic material from the Hobbs site indicate the region has been used for several thousand years.

Moving up the Spanish system into the central region, the archaeological record reflects the dichotomy between travel along the rivers and life on the interior lakes. This area is also above glacial Lake Nipissing and skirts along the shores of Lake Algonquin. Both these factors will give the archaeological record a different complexion than is evident on the lower river.

Gough or Birch Lake is part of the traditional Spanish River canoe route. The lake is connected east to the elbow of Agnew Lake by a portage that runs four to five kilometers along a series of creeks. Traveling south from Gough Lake, the portage to the lower Spanish followed the Birch Creek outlet. Portaging west through Gough Lake, travellers were able to avoid the 33 k jog the Spanish makes to the east, including the portages around High Falls at the eastern end of Agnew Lake and Espanola Falls at Espanola,

Ontario. The early historic use of the Gough Lake route is documented on Chief Factor John McBean's 1827 map (Fig. 2) (PAC, HBCA, D. 5/2, fo. 257). Dominic Eshkakogan and Alex Sago of Sagamok, both remember their grandfathers talking about an Ojibwa village located on Gough Lake in the nineteenth century (1980: personal communication).

No comprehensive archaeological survey of Gough Lake has been done. As a result, the link between the archaeological record and oral history on the lake has not been firmly established. The MCC conducted a limited investigation of a small redeposited prehistoric site (CbHl-1) on the north side of the lake in 1980. The site has been eroded by artificially high water levels caused by a Ministry of Natural Resources dam. CbHl-1 appears to date from the Middle Woodland period. Identification of the Middle Woodland occupation was made by Thor Conway, based upon a single grit-tempered body sherd (1980: personal communication). The lithic assemblage contains both chert and quartzite scrapers, gravers and a white quartzite flake knife. Interestingly the knife is a very fine grained, milky white quartzite with green inclusions and a waxy finish that in some ways resembles the Rama quartzite from Labrador. Whether or not the flake knife is Rama quartzite is not the question. What really matters in terms of understanding the archaeology of the region is that the material is an exotic substance that does not occur locally. Additionally, a flake of jasper taconite was also found on the site. Taconite is very common on the northwest shore of Lake Superior near Thunder Bay, Ontario. Small quantities of taconite are evident on Point aux Pins along the St. Mary's River, at Sault Ste Marie. It is quite rare along the north shore of Lake Huron. The presence of exotic materials at CbHl-1 from Middle Woodland times links the Spanish into a prehistoric inter-regional trade system that extends from the western Great Lakes to Quebec.

Moving north along the Spanish there is a series of small prehistoric sites on the banks of the river. At the portage around an old cataract at the head of Agnew Lake, a lithic scatter was excavated by the INCo Spanish River survey in 1980 (Hanks 1981:150–75). A small pocket of charcoal found in association with quartzite bifacial thinning flakes produced a date of $5,910 \pm 115$ B.P. (I-11,699) (Hanks 1981:203). CcHl-2 appears to represent a single episode. Two overlapping clusters of large quartzite bifacial thinning flakes indicate that substantial quartzite bifaces were refitted.

Immediately upstream from CcHl-2, stands Eagle Rock. According to John and Alex Sago, there are crevasse burials along the face of the rock (1980: personal communication). Thor Conway maintains that this is the most northerly report of the Ottawa type of cave burial (1987: personal communication).

Four kilometers upstream from Agnew Lake, a single large reworked quartzite flake was located on the surface (CcHl-1). CcHl-3 is situated across

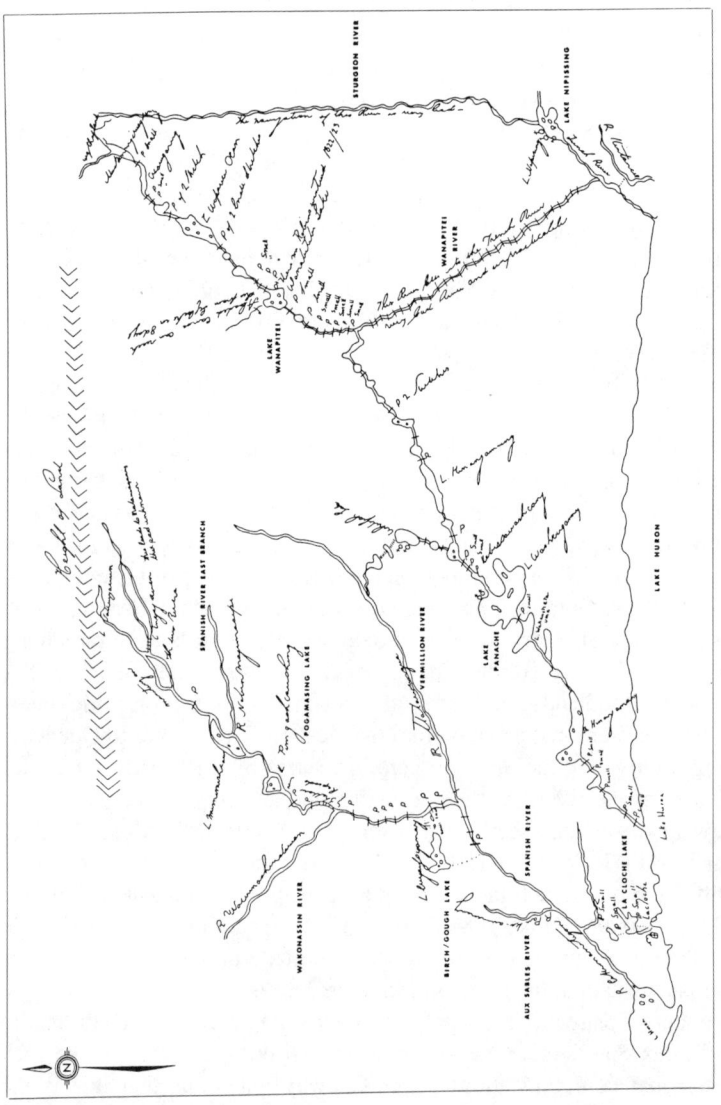

Figure 2. 1827 McBean map of the north shore of Lake Huron.

from the junction of the Wakonassin River. Preliminary testing revealed a wide distribution of quartz flakes (Hanks 1981:53).

Forty kilometers north of Agnew Lake, Sinaminda Lake drains into the Spanish from the west via Agnes Creek. CfHl-1 was located by MCC. The assemblage consists of a fragment of a large white quartzite biface and a hammerstone. As with Gough Lake, no systematic survey has been done of the lake. This single small site does, however, support the theory that people moved from the rivers into the large isolated interior lakes.

Continuing up the Spanish into the Graveyard Rapids, CdHk-2 yielded a very small collection of flakes. It is located on the portage around the third cataract (Hanks 1981:95–96). Several kilometers upstream, at the elbow of the Spanish River, CdHk-1 sits at the head of the portage to Fox Lake. A single trihedral adze was found on the surface.

CdHk-3–5 on Fox Lake produced a sequence that ranged from the Early Archaic (ca. 7600 B.P.) to the Late Woodland. These sites are given a much more in-depth treatment later on in the analysis.

Eleven kilometers above the elbow the river widens out into Spanish Lake. CeHk-1 is located on the northeast corner of the lake. The site is located on an open bedrock slope. The assemblage consists of black chert and quartz flakes. This appears to represent a single episode (Hanks 1981:127). CeHk-2 is situated on the east side of Spanish Lake. Two kaolin pipe stems stamped with the initials TD on their tangs probably represent a mid-nineteenth century occupation. The prehistoric component consists of a corner-notched projectile point, a broken ground polished celt, a bladelike Hudson's Bay Lowland chert biface, and chert flakes. Based upon a comparison of the projectile point with Wright's Shield Archaic (1972) and the Laurentian Archaic (Ritchie 1980:72), this site has been tentatively assigned to the Late Archaic, that is, 4000 to 2500 B.P. (Hanks 1981:135).

Thirty kilometers north of Spanish Lake and one kilometer west of the Spanish River lies Pogamasing Lake. Once again, only preliminary survey work has been done on this lake. The old Hudson's Bay Company post (CfHk-3) was located on Kingsley Island. It was open from the 1880s into the early twentieth century (PAC, HBCA, D.25/4, fo. 70). Three ground stone celts found on the island by a local lodge owner, also indicate an undefined prehistoric occupation. Site CfHk-4 is located on the premises of Butchard's camp lodge. Like many sites in the drainage, preliminary investigation revealed a nonceramic assemblage. The collection consists of a side-notched projectile point, three thumbnail-sized end scrapers, a bipolar blade and numerous chert flakes. The single side-notched projectile point is nondescript enough that it could be either Late Archaic or Middle Woodland in origin (Hanks 1981:145).

Arriving at the upper end of the Spanish drainage, 17 prehistoric sites have been recorded on Biscotasing Lake. The majority of these were found by wildlife officers from Chapleau (John Pollock 1981: personal communication). These sites have never been written up and little is known about them.

Briefly, the patchwork of archaeology done in the Spanish drainage over the years has revealed an occupation which stretches over 7000 years. The presence of exotic raw materials (e.g., taconite, Hudson's Bay Lowland chert, nonlocal quartzite and gray and black cherts which at least visually resemble material from the Upper Peninsula of Michigan) suggest long distance trade. This ties the Spanish River canoe route into the movement of people and goods between the Great Lakes and the interior at least over the last two to three thousand years. Conversely, the Early Archaic assemblages at CcHl-2 and CdHk-3 are entirely made of local quartz, quartzite and graywacke.

Though work on all the lakes but Fox is at a preliminary stage, a review of the archaeology reveals larger interior lake sites that probably represent occupation sites as opposed to the very small travel camps found along the river. To extrapolate from the historic period, prehistoric peoples probably also went down to Lake Huron to exploit the fall fishery and withdrew into the interior to hunt during the winter. This suggests trade and shifting seasonal patterns of subsistence are the motivating forces behind human movement between the interior and the Lake Huron plain.

## Location of CdHk-3

The Foxie Otter site (CdHk-3) is located on the shore of Fox Lake approximately 88 k north of Sudbury, Ontario (Fig. 1). The site is situated on the northwest corner of the lake on the premises of the Fox Lake Lodge, and is over one hectare in size. It extends along the base of two bays, separated by a peninsula which adjoins Otter Slide Island. The site's present geomorphology has been altered by artificially high water levels caused by a logger's dam built in the 1930s. The dam is now maintained by Ontario's Ministry of Natural Resources, to control the water flow in John's Creek. As a result of the high water level, a part of CdHk-3 along the northeast segment of the site now lies under an artificial bay. Otter Slide Island was formerly part of the northeast shore of the lake. It is now connected to the mainland by a narrow isthmus. Erosion along the banks of Otter Slide Island and the mainland are slowly causing parts of the site to slip into the lake.

Fox Lake is connected to the Spanish River drainage system by the John's Creek. The lake is situated approximately two kilometers from the elbow in the Spanish River. At pre-dam lake levels, CdHk-3 would have been at the head of Fox Lake and at the natural terminus for the portage from the Spanish River. Logically, access to Fox Lake from the Spanish River was probably gained by the portage from the elbow, and not by the longer, and shallow, John's Creek.

## History of Research at CdHk-3

The Foxie Otter site was found by Nick Adams of the INCo Spanish River survey during the fall of 1980. A preliminary surface survey was carried out at the site and three one-meter-square units were excavated. As Fox Lake was outside the INCo study area, an extensive survey of the lake was not conducted in 1980.

In 1981, I returned to the site to conduct further excavation with the aid of a grant from the Ontario Heritage Foundation. During a five-week field season in late May and June of 1981, the property of the Fox Lake Lodge was surveyed and 22 one-meter-square units were excavated. Due to the restricted period of time available for field research and several days of bad weather, field work was restricted to CdHk-3. As a result, the rest of Fox Lake was not systematically surveyed at that time.

The net result of the 1980 and 1981 research at the Foxie Otter site has been the surface and subsurface testing of the site, the preparation of a contour map, and the excavation of 25 square meters of cultural deposits.

Additional work has been done on Fox Lake by Ken Buchanan of the Archaeological Survey of Laurentian University, Sudbury. This research yielded two small sites (CdHk-13 and -14) approximately one kilometer southwest of CdHk-3 (Devereux 1982: personal communication). On the basis of lithic samples of graywacke and the debitage from CdHk-13, it was postulated that there was a similarity to Foxie Otter. According to Buchanan and Devereux, both CdHk-13 and -14 are at the water's edge or under water. Investigation of the garden immediately behind CdHk-13 yielded no traces of occupation (Devereux 1982: personal communication).

The archaeological remains nearest to Fox Lake on the Spanish River are located at the elbow (CdHk-1), where a single trihedral adze was found on the surface by the INCo survey (Hanks 1981:89). The significance of CdHk-1, in relation to CdHk-3, is its location at the other end of the Fox Lake portage, and the trihedral adze which is chronologically comparable to the Early Archaic component found at CdHk-3. Research to date has made a significant step toward providing a basis for the interpretation of the prehistoric occupation of the Fox Lake area. The subsequent analysis of CdHk-3 will provide a foundation upon which others working in the region can build.

# 2
# GEOLOGY AND REGIONAL PALEOENVIRONMENT

## Bedrock Geology and Lithic Sources

The topography of the Spanish River–Fox Lake region is relatively flat. Fox Lake is in a valley ringed by outcrop hills and glacio-lacustrine deposits averaging 50 meters in height. The outlet of the lake is to the northeast through a cut in a gravel plain left by the postglacial course of the Spanish River. Drainage around the lake is poor, resulting in frequent swamps and small ponds.

Bedrock deposits in the Upper Spanish drainage contain a variety of raw materials that were frequently used by the prehistoric inhabitants of the area for the production of stone tools. The geologic structure of the Spanish River drainage has been summarized by J. J. Hannila:

> [The] area is underlain by granite-quartz-monzonite rocks of the Early Precambrian age. A wedge of Middle Precambrian-Huronian age conglomerate, quartzite and siltstone of the Gowganda formation lies unconformable on the granitic basement in the northern part of the area. Numerous Middle to Late Precambrian gabbro-diabase sills and dykes intrude the sediments and granites. A blanket of Pleistocene and recent gravel deposits cover a large part of the area. [1979:A]

Exposed Huronian-age Gowganda-formation quartzite, conglomerates (e.g., graywacke) and siltstones found near Fox Lake are represented in the tool assemblage at CdHk-3. In addition to the local materials, cherts that visually resemble material from northern Michigan and the Hudson Bay Lowlands are present in the Woodland component at the site.

## Pleistocene Geology

Fox Lake was deglaciated at the end of the Valder's Advance, ten to eleven thousand years ago (Kam and Davis 1981:1). The headwaters of the Spanish River were ice-free shortly after 9500 B.P. (Kelly and Farrand 1967:15–16). While the ice withdrew to the north of the Lake Huron basin around 11,000 B.P., a local readvance moved across southern Ontario blocking the Trent

Valley outlet. The closure of the Trent caused glacial Lake Algonquin to rise to the 605 foot (184.4 meter) level (Kelly and Farrand 1967:15) flooding the Spanish River system and turning it into an arm of Lake Algonquin as far north as Spanish Lake. The fossil beach lines of glacial Lake Algonquin, are found today at approximately 335 meters (1,099 ft. a.s.l.) on the Spanish River and John's Creek valleys (Spanish River Feasibility Report 1978:6). Despite the differential rate at which rebound occurs north of Lake Huron, a beach formation has been tentatively identified eight kilometers north of Fox Lake on the Jack Pine Flats of the Spanish River. This formation is at about the 1,100 foot (335 m) contour. As such, it is probably a result of glacial Lake Algonquin, but only intensive geomorphological work in the area will resolve the precise penetration of postglacial lakes.

With the retreat of Lake Algonquin, the east branch of the Spanish River became a minor spillway for glacial waters backed up behind the Cartier II moraine (Boissonneau 1968:102). As a consequence of the glacial retreat, inundation of Lake Algonquin and outwash deposits from the period of the Lake Sultan spillway, low-lying areas less than 800 feet, are overlaid with massive deposits of lacustrine clay. Overlaying the clay on the edge of the Precambrian Shield along the upland's edge on a transect from Bruce Mines to Capreol are silt and deltaic deposits between 800 to 1100 feet in elevation (e.g., fossil remains of Nipissing and Algonquin shorelines). The most conspicuous glacio-lacustrine deposits are composed of sand and gravel (Boissonneau 1968:102). In the Spanish River system, it was the erosion of moraine and lacustrine sand and gravel deposits which formed the uneven terrace system.

Approximately 11,000 B.P., the Spanish River flowed directly into John's Creek over a low bedrock sill between the elbow of the Spanish River and Fox Lake at the head of the John's. As the glacial flood waters subsided causing increased gradients and down cutting, the Spanish River abandoned the John's Creek route and turned westward at the elbow and swung back to the south through the Graveyard Rapids (Spanish River Feasibility Report 1978:6). This is the modern course of the Spanish River.

After the retreat of Algonquin, circa 10,000 B.P., the water level in the Lake Huron basin dropped dramatically during the Lake Stanley stage to a low of 190 feet (Hough 1966:75). By about 6000 B.P., the water had risen to the 605 foot level of postglacial Lake Nipissing (Boissoneau 1968:108 and Hough 1966:75). On Manitoulin Island the Nipissing shoreline is at approximately 198 m (649 ft.) a.s.l. at Britainville, and 214 m (699 ft.) a.s.l. at Killarney on the north shore of Lake Huron (Lewis 1970:672). Given the faster rate of rebound north of Lake Huron, the Nipissing shoreline in the Spanish drainage should be slightly above the 214 m (669 ft.) level at Killarney. Despite the lack of a precise location for the Lake Nipissing shoreline near Massey and Espanola, Ontario, evidence in adjoining areas indicates that it should be found between 214 m (669 ft.) a.s.l. and the edge of the Canadian Shield. After the Nipissing stage, the water level in the Lake Huron basin receded to the Lake Algoma stage at a present elevation of 187 m (610 ft.). The Lake Algoma stage has been dated to $4080 \pm 130$ B.P.(GSC-301) (Boissonneau 1968:108) on the basis of wood charcoal found in lacustrine sand near Massey, Ontario.

Archaic sites south of Spanish Lake in the central Spanish system are on or below the Algonquin levels, and inland from the Nipissing-Algoma beaches. The Hobbs site on the Aux Sables River in the lower drainage is near the level of Algoma waters. These factors become significant when the traditional beach ridge approach to surveying for Early Archaic assemblages is considered. The standard beach ridge intuitive model of site distribution must be expanded to include inland utilization.

## Paleoclimate

At around 11,300 B.P. a major change was noted in the pollen frequencies of the Minnesota-Wisconsin region. That warming trend has been characterized by Ogden (1977:19) as having these characteristics:

1. Increased duration of Pacific south air in winter and predominance during July.
2. Increase in summer season (maritime tropical air) of one month.
3. Increase in length of growing season degree days, along with approximately 3.3 degrees C increase in July mean temperature.
4. Decline of snowfall and cloudiness.

This climatic amelioration is evident in the Loon Lake pollen diagrams (Kam and Davis 1981). Loon Lake is approximately 15 kilometers northeast of Fox Lake. The close proximity of Loon Lake to CdHk-3 allows accurate climatic reconstruction of the Fox Lake area. The Cartier morainic belt, within which Loon Lake is located, was deglaciated during the period 11,000 to 10,100 B.P. (Kam and Davis 1981:1). The basal organic layer at Loon Lake produced a radiocarbon date of $10,230 \pm 200$ B.P. (Kam and Davis 1981:3). Kam and Davis accept this date as comparable with the deglaciation chronology and the regeneration of the flora (1981:1). In contradiction to Cleland's (1966) proposed tundra-like environment of grasses and sedges for the upper Great Lakes, Kam and Davis's pollen data "...show no clear evidence of tundra during the late-glacial" period (1981:2). In the period immediately following deglaciation, a forest dominated by spruce (*Picea*) with traces of jack pine (*Pinus*) and white birch (*Betula alba*) was present at Loon Lake (Kam and Davis 1981:2). With the draining of Lake Algonquin through the North Bay/proto-Ottawa Valley around 10,000 B.P., a similar sequence of rapid forest development characterized the Sheguiandah site on Manitoulin Island (Ogden 1977:25–26). As Sheguiandah emerged from under Lake Algonquin it experienced a relatively rapid forest development. The basal layer of peat, dated at $9130 \pm 250$ B.P., is characterized by the appearance of both spruce *(Picea)* and pine *(Pinus)* (Lee 1957:118). This sequence for Sheguiandah's development is compatible with the Loon Lake data which also indicate a decline in spruce and the advance of jack pine and white birch by around 9200 B.P.(Kam and Davis 1981:2). Both the Loon Lake and Sheguiandah data are in line with a general warming trend that began around $10,275 \pm 520$ B.P. from Minnesota to Nova Scotia (Ogden 1977:19).

The boreal forest southeast of Lake Superior declined and was replaced by white pine between approximately $8830 \pm 200$ B.P. and $7630 \pm 180$ B.P. (Saarnisto 1975:307). At Loon Lake, the boreal spruce forest declined during this time to be replaced by white birch and jack pine which in turn were rapidly displaced by white pine in the period immediately after 7700 B.P. (Kam and Davis 1981:2). During the white pine maximum, the boreal species reached their lowest population levels while thermophilous species such as hemlock *(Tsuga)* and beech *(Fagus)* moved into the region forming the basis from which the mixed hardwood of the Lake Forest were established (Kam and Davis 1981:2; Ritchie 1980:82; Fitting 1975:28). The period of the white pine maximum, circa 7700–4300 B.P., coincided with the time of maximum postglacial warming and dryness known as the xerotheric or hypsithermal (Cleland 1966:21, Kam and Davis 1981:2). During the hypsithermal, the boreal and Great Lake-St. Lawrence forest ecotones were north of their present limits (Kam and Davis 1981:2).

Around 6300 B.P. a final glacial advance occurred in the Cochrane area of northern Ontario (Boissonneau 1966:576). In light of the most recent palynological evidence, the Cochrane Advance does not appear to have altered the postglacial climatic amelioration that was occurring in the upper Great Lakes region at that time (McAndrews 1981: personal communication). A climatic cooling began around 4300 B.P. and intensified after 2800 B.P. resulting in a decline in white pine, while boreal species such as spruce, jack pine and white birch increased in the Loon Lake region.

Though climate certainly does not preordain adaptive options, it does influence choices. When rapid climatic change occurs, as it did in the postglacial period, people would have been forced to adapt quickly to survive. This variability of climatic circumstance is evident in the two dated sites which have been excavated in the Spanish River drainage: CdHk-3 ($7670 \pm 120$ B.P.) and CcHl-2 at Agnew Lake ($5910 \pm 115$ B.P.) (Hanks 1981:150–75). At the time CdHk-3 was occupied, the ice sheet still extended below James Bay. Though the climate had undergone amelioration, the pine forests had only recently taken hold in the region as it emerged from a subarctic environment. By the time CcHl-2 was inhabited, the climate was at the height of the hypsithermal and the Cochrane Advance had passed. These climatic differences undoubtedly affected the types of resources available and hence human adaptation.

Our lack of knowledge about the Early Archaic in the upper Great Lakes is, to a large extent, due to the rapid decrease and subsequent increases in proto-Huron water levels. The lack of documented sites for this period makes the Foxie Otter site important, as it can substantially increase our knowledge about human adaptation during this critical period of postglacial change.

# 3
# HISTORY OF FIELD RESEARCH AND METHODOLOGY

The Foxie Otter site was first discovered in the fall of 1980. After the initial discovery, a preliminary survey was conducted along eroding segments of the shoreline, and trails and roads used by Fox Lake Lodge. This surface and subsurface investigation located four archaeological loci: area E, south of the Otter Slide cabin; area D, between the old dock crib and the driveway on the east side of the site; area C, to the west of the Moose Run cabin in the center of the site; and area A, along the cut driveway leading to the Scaler's Camp dock on the northern edge of CdHk-3 (Hanks 1981:102) (see Fig. 3). The discovery of four large graywacke bifaces and an end scraper on the bank of the east shore (area D) prompted the excavation of three one-meter units during 1980 (Hanks 1981:100).

Because the east bank had been disturbed by a cottage being dragged across it, the surface layer of humus was gone. The disturbance of natural soil levels led to the decision to excavate the units in two-centimeter arbitrary levels. The units were excavated in a short transect through the eroding slope into the area where the concentration of graywacke flakes had been observed. Unit 10N0E was found to be totally disturbed; 10N1W and 10N2W had intact podzol horizons, but the humus was removed. A small pit feature at the base of the podzol was found to contain charcoal in association with graywacke flakes (Hanks 1981:102). On the basis of that dated feature and the extensive remains found elsewhere on the site, it was decided to return to CdHk-3 in 1981. Our goal was to define the extent of the site and to recover more of the Early Archaic component located the year before. Upon returning to the site, excavation was begun of three one-meter units in natural levels near the Moose Run cabin (area C). This location was chosen for immediate examination because in 1980 graywacke flakes had been located on the surface. In area D, graywacke flakes had been found in association with feature 1 in 1980. This feature was subsequently dated to the Early Archaic. The rationale for commencing the excavation in area C was to find another concentration that might be associated with the Early Archaic occupation. An *in situ* clay-walled hearth feature was found in unit B-0, but there was no cultural material in association with it. Located stratigraphically above the hearth, at the base of the humus, in the same unit was a seed bead. The historic bead

20                    *Foxie Otter Site*

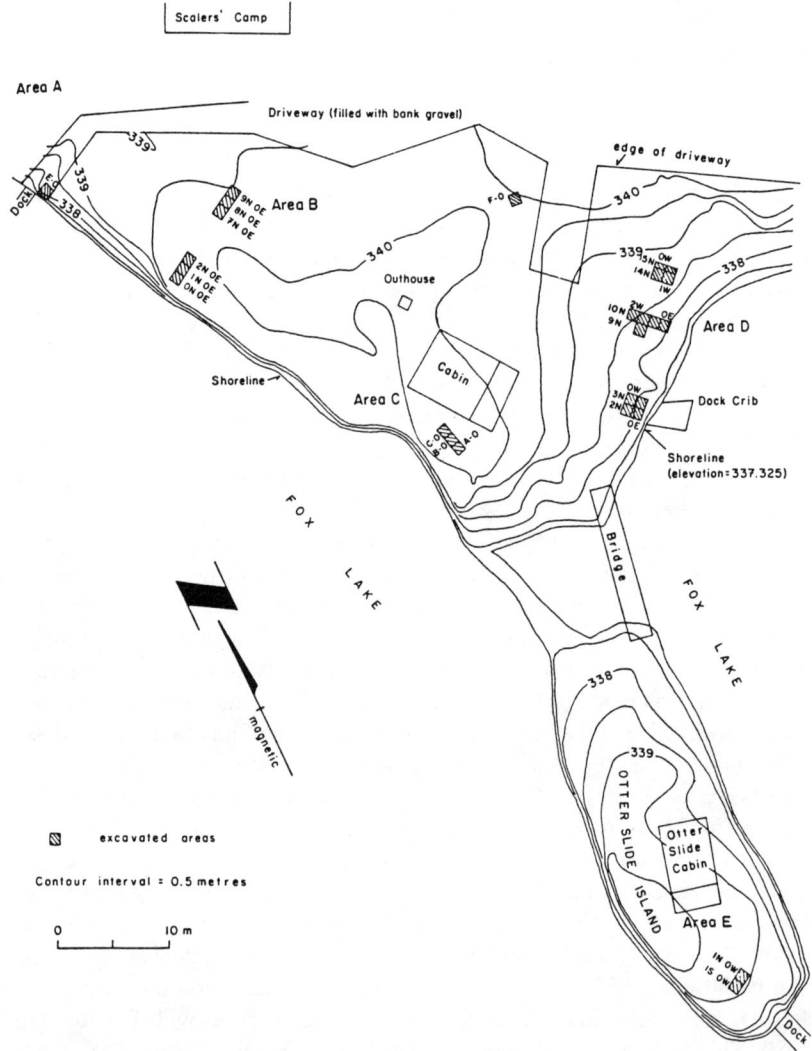

Figure 3. The Foxie Otter site, CdHk-3.

and the hearth are in visibly different levels. At least in this area, there is vertical stratigraphy. At this time, however, carbon samples from this distinct feature have not been dated because there were no artifacts in association.

After the excavation of area C, a formal transect survey was conducted on the known site. Transects were spaced four meters apart. On each line, 30-centimeter test pits were placed at four-meter intervals. Five positive tests were found. Three were situated along the driveway in area A, while the other two were located in area B. These later test pits were subsequently subsumed in units 0N0E and 8N0E.

As a result of the survey area B was discovered. This filled a blank in the site along the head of the bay between areas A and C. In order to define the extent of remains in area B, six one-meter-square units were excavated in natural levels. These units revealed a diffuse but extensive prehistoric cultural horizon in the 2 to 3 cm thick podzol zone. If further work is done at CdHk-3, the extension of the units adjoining the six one-meter squares in area B should be given a high priority.

Despite the large number of flakes collected from the surface of area A, only limited excavation was undertaken because of the extensive disturbance caused by the road cut. One one-meter square was placed at the edge of the slumping bank, where the road meets the dock. Unit E-0 was selected because of a surface concentration of quartzite flakes. The unit was capped by B-horizon soil which had been leveled across it as a result of road work. Excavation was by natural levels. A hearth feature was found folded into a slumpage caused by wave action. Though the stratigraphy was mixed, the podzol layer was intact enough to map the hearth and its associated artifacts.

It is obvious that the cultural material present in area A is not isolated to the driveway area. If further work is done on the site, units should be excavated on either side of the driveway.

Area E is located on the south end of Otter Slide Island. The first surface finds were made along the eroding bank on the southwest corner of the island. Units 1N0W and 1S0W were placed to the east of the bank in an area that has suffered disturbance from foot traffic. The cultural horizon is located in the podzol. This layer is two to three centimeters thick and is underlain by sterile B-horizon soils. Humus and podzol layers on Otter Slide Island are very thin. Material within these two layers has undergone extensive movement due to human and natural factors (e.g., a very heavy root mat).

Since the discovery of Early Archaic material on the surface of area D, 12 one-meter units have been excavated to try and define the component. This sector of the site is on a slope that has been extensively disturbed by natural and human forces. Despite this, extensive concentrations of lithic debris have been recovered in undisturbed strata. These discoveries have been made by carefully wedging units in between disturbed areas. While there may be more cultural material in area D, it is unlikely to be *in situ*.

Furthermore, much of area D is now under water. Both CdHk-13 and -14 were also found at the water's edge (Devereux 1982: personal communication). This evidence demonstrates the impact of artificially high water levels on sites along Fox Lake. If further work is conducted, it should concentrate on other sectors of the site.

Organic samples were collected in the form of faunal remains, soil samples for flotation, and charcoal for fractionation. Faunal remains on the site are not abundant (Appendix 1). A total of 18 soil samples were obtained for flotation. These samples were submitted to the botany department of the Royal Ontario Museum for analysis (Appendix 2). Eleven carbon samples including the 1980 date on the Archaic component, have been recovered (Appendix 3). Nine of these samples have been assayed at the present time. The organic remains are discussed more fully in the appropriate sections of the analysis.

Units were dug in both arbitrary and natural levels depending upon the integrity of the ground surface. One-meter squares divided into quadrants were used as the basic excavation unit. Adjoining squares were separated by baulks 10 centimeters wide to control stratigraphy. Artifacts were plotted three dimensionally and bagged by quadrant and level. Excavation by natural levels was a more successful technique in areas where there was not intensive disturbance. Surface disruption led to the use of arbitrary levels in some sectors of area D. Careful recording made it possible to reconcile the natural and artificial levels in the laboratory. The circumstances under which the original discoveries were made justified the initial use of arbitrary levels as a means for controlling exploratory excavation.

The shore of both bays at the old head of the lake underwent controlled surface and subsurface testing. Twenty-five one-meter squares were excavated. As CdHk-3 is over a hectare in size, only a small portion of the site has been tested as of this writing. The judgmental and transect sampling strategy used in this study has roughly defined the parameters of at least two broad periods of occupation (Early Archaic and Late Woodland/Contact). Future research should include a transect survey north of area A and block excavations in areas A, B, and C. Area B has the most known undisturbed strata. Heavy disturbance in area D eliminates the need for further investigation in that sector. Survey to the northwest of area A may well reveal additional concentrations of undisturbed remains.

In summary, research at CdHk-3 has documented the presence of historic, Woodland and Archaic occupations of the site. Eroding areas were investigated and recorded. These studies point out the need for continued research at the site. Additional field work would allow a more geographically representative sample to be obtained and elucidate the areal distribution of features across CdHk-3.

# 4
# THE ANALYSIS OF CDHK-3

The analysis of the archaeological remains at CdHk-3 is presented in three segments: features; production and maintenance of stone tools; and the relationship between features and lithic processes.

## Dating the Features

Features and artifacts at CdHk-3 were dated on two levels. First, tentative ages were assigned on the basis of artifact associations. Second, these estimates were compared to dated C-14 samples. All of the dated samples were charcoal obtained from hearths.

Nine of the eleven carbon samples recovered have been processed. Eight samples obtained in 1981 were processed by the laboratory at Simon Fraser University. The sample obtained in 1980 was dated at Teledyne Isotopes. Two remaining samples are from hearths in unit B-0. It is hoped that these remaining samples will be processed in the future.

A number of considerations were taken into account in evaluating the carbon dates from CdHk-3. First is the strength of association between the samples and the cultural remains with which they were found. Second, how reliable were the various samples as datable material? Finally, are the uncalibrated dates comparable with the sequences proposed on the site?

The degree of association between material culture and dated cultural features is the essence of the dating process. H. T. Waterbalk (1971) defines four levels of positive correlation between dated and cultural material: (1) *full certainty*, where a cultural artifact is dated; (2) *high probability*, where a direct functional relationship exists; (3) *probability* where no functional relationship exists, but the quantity of material argues for a relationship; and (4) *reasonable possibility* where there is a reasonable proximity, such as charcoal flecks in an occupation floor (1971:16). Applying these criteria to the Foxie Otter dates, it was found that none of the relationships were stronger than a probability (Table 1). The most satisfactory associations are I-11,700, in which dated charcoal and flakes were found in direct association within a pit, and SFU-153 and -151, which were taken from hearths with flakes mixed in the charcoal. A second group, still classed as a probability, has an associa-

TABLE 1
Carbon 14 Dates from CdHk-3

| Date | Sample No. | Provenience |
|---|---|---|
| 170 ± 120 B.P. | SFU 152 | ScE 1N0E Q 3 L 2 |
| 370 ± 90 B.P. | SFU 153 | ScE 0N0W Q 2 L 2 F 4 |
| 480 ± 260 B.P. | SFU 169 | OS 0N0W Q 2 L 3 F 7 |
| 610 ± 80 B.P. | SFU 154 | ScE E-0 Q 4 L 4 F 3 |
| 690 ± 180 B.P. | SFU 151 | ScE 1N0W Q 4 L 2 F 4 |
| 1320 ± 700 B.P. | SFU 170 | 38B 14N0W Q 2 L 2 F 6 |
| 1450 ± 250 B.P. | SFU 155 | ScE 1N0W Q 1 L 2 F 4 |
| 1840 ± 350 B.P. | SFU 171 | OS 1S0W Q 1 L 3 |
| 7670 ± 120 B.P. | I-11,700 | 38B 10N2W Q 2 L 2-3 F D |

ScE = Scaler's Camp East grid
OS = Otter Slide Island grid
38B = 38° baseline grid
00N00E or W = references the square to the local datum established for each of the three major grids
Q = quadrants 1–4 of the 1 m squares
L = natural soil levels
F = feature number

tion which is not quite as clear. This includes samples SFU-169, -170, -154 and -155, which were taken from disturbed hearths with flakes in association with charcoal. The final group consists of dates where a reasonable possibility of association exists but is not as direct. Samples SFU-152 and -171 were collected from flecks of charcoal collected in disturbed lenses presumed to be hearths with cultural material in loose association. Dates resulting from these two samples are more tenuous than those taken from more distinct pit and hearth features. None of the material culture has "highly probable" associations with dated samples. Seven of the nine samples, however, are from clearly recognizable features where there exists a good probability that the dates are associated with human occupation. The remaining two samples are from diffuse charcoal lens only assumed to be in association with human occupation. Consequently, the dates from SFU-152 and SFU-171 will only be considered if they fall within the range of other dates from CdHk-3.

Samples size is critical to obtaining reliable dates. Though a date can be obtained on as little as two grams of carbon, a much larger quantity is desirable (Huntley 1981:1.10). The actual size of the specimen required depends on the material in question. Wood charcoal, which was the substance used for dating at CdHk-3, should have a collected sample size of at least 25 grams to allow for adequate cleaning (Huntley 1981:1.11, 1.12). With the exception of I-11,700, which contained 40 grams of wood charcoal, all the other samples were between 10 and 15 grams in size. Specimen I-11,700 was cleaned with both hydrochloric acid (HCl) to remove inorganic substances and sodium hydroxide (NaOH) to reduce humic acid (Buckley 1980: personal communication; Huntley 1981:1.13). Samples SFU-151, -152, -153, -154, -155, -169, -170 and -171 were cleaned with HCl but were too small for treatment with NaOH (Hobson 1982: personal communication; Hobson and Nelson 1983:904). As these specimens were not treated with NaOH, it is likely that significant quantities of humic acid could have been part of the dated material. This factor, and the small sample size, may account for the large standard deviations exhibited by several of the samples (Hobson 1982: personal communication).

The shallow depth of the archaeological deposits and the forested environment make the problem of humic acid critical in evaluating the dates. Further, compressed stratigraphy compounds the possibility that admixture occurred between naturally and culturally produced carbon. As a result of these factors, it is unrealistic to accept the carbon dates uncritically. On balance, few if any dates from sites in the northern forests are free of similar problems.

Given these considerations, it is wiser to think of the range of dates present than to emphasize individual samples. This rule holds true except in the case of the proposed Archaic component where only one date has been accepted. Fortunately I-11,700 is the one sample which was sealed well below the humus layer, properly cleaned and double assayed. Despite the acceptance of the soundness of this sample, it is still presumptuous to put too much weight on a single specimen. A second sample SFU-170 (1320 ± 700) was removed from a proposed hearth feature in association with graywacke debitage. At the time it was collected, it was hypothesized to be Archaic in origin. Regrettably, the sample was very small (less than 10 grams). After cleaning with HCl the lab did not feel there was a large enough specimen left to be able to apply the NaOH treatment. The extremely large standard deviation may be attributed to humic acid concentrations in the sample (Hobson 1982: personal communication). As a result of that factor, it is reasonable to reject the date (Hobson 1982: personal communication). Sample SFU-152 (170 ± 120 B.P.) was also rejected because of an excessively large standard deviation relative to the mean date.

Despite large standard deviations on several other samples, it was decided to consider the rest of the dates in this interpretation of CdHk-3. The remaining six dates all fall within the Woodland period. They range from Transitional to Late/Terminal Woodland times. Individually, they are not extremely reliable but, as a group they do present some potentially useful patterns.

The final factor in dating CdHk-3 is the comparison of the artifact assemblage with the sequence proposed on the basis of the carbon dates. It was hypothesized prior to the carbon dating that the samples would yield Woodland dates ranging between A.D. 600 and A.D. 1450–1500. This is based upon an interpretation of the artifacts which include a small thin sherd of grit-tempered pottery, two side-notched projectile points identified as Transitional Woodland, and a small triangular point classed as Late Woodland (Conway and Wright 1982: personal communication). The large graywacke bifaces and the end scraper are not on their own diagnostic of any given period. The typological uniqueness of the graywacke assemblage and carbon date I-11,700 (7620 ± 120 B.P.), however, were used in conjunction to identify the Early Archaic (ca. 8000–5500 B.P.) occupation. Because none of the carbon samples were found in direct association with chronologically diagnostic artifacts, it is impossible to link specific artifact forms with any of the dates.

A cultural sequence can be proposed for CdHk-3 by comparing the dates with one another, documenting patterns within these dates, and drawing analogies with the limited collection of chronologically diagnostic artifacts.

It was decided to compare the dates from CdHk-3 using a $t$ distribution. A $t$ statistic can be used to question whether two dates are truly different or if the variability between them can be accounted for by statistical error (Thomas 1976:250). In light of the small samples and the resulting large standard deviations, the necessity of separating statistical error from actual age differences between the carbon samples is critical to the interpretation. The test assumes as a null hypothesis that the two dates are related and that the variability is due to statistical error. The null hypothesis will be rejected in a two-tailed $t$ test at the .05 level with a score of greater than or equal to ±1.96 with infinite degrees of freedom (Thomas 1976:250).

The comparison indicates three unrelated clusters of dates. The first group contains samples SFU-153, -169, -154 and -151, which comprise a range of dates between A.D. 1260 and 1580 representing the Late or Terminal Woodland occupation on the site.

A second cluster represented by SFU samples 155 and 171 indicates a possible occupation during the period A.D 100–500. However, artifactual evidence from CdHk-3 does not support a Middle Woodland occupation. The oldest Woodland artifacts on the site are a pair of side-notched projectile points that J. V. Wright and Thor Conway have indicated are Transitional Woodland from the period around A.D. 700 to 1000 (1981: personal communication). This cluster of dates does not represent an occupation that has been corroborated by any other evidence from the site. It is, therefore, reasonable to assume that either these dates represent a forest fire lens or a cultural horizon that has yet to be defined.

The final cluster contains sample I-11,700, which has been dated at 7670 ± 120 B.P. or approximately 5720 B.C. The Early Archaic affiliation of this date is confirmed typologically at the site. Corroborating evidence for the Early Archaic can be found regionally at CdHk-1 in the form of a trihedral adze. CdHk-1 is located 2 kilometers from CdHk-3, at the elbow of the Spanish River (Hanks 1982:92). Tony Buchner has tentatively dated trihedral adzes found at the Sinnock site in southeastern Manitoba at around 6000 B.C. or 8000 B.P (1981:68). Trihedral adzes in northwestern Ontario are considered to have an early Shield Archaic context between 4000 and 6000

B.C., or 6000 and 8000 B.P. (Fox 1980:123). Despite this supporting evidence there still exists but a single C-14 date. It would be presumptuous to claim, on the basis of that date, that the Early Archaic component has been firmly defined.

The carbon dates from CdHk-3 indicate the presence of two cultural horizons and a probable forest fire. CdHk-3 was undoubtedly occupied more extensively than the dates indicate. The dates do, however, document the existence of multiple components at the site.

## Archaeobotanical Analysis

The archaeobotanical remains from the Foxie Otter site were not extensive, but they do provide some insight into the occupation. Rodolphe Fecteau and John McAndrews of the Royal Ontario Museum have analyzed the organic remains from CdHk-3. Their report has been included in Appendix 2. To avoid repetition, this section of the analysis will concentrate only upon those botanical remains which have a direct effect upon the interpretation of CdHk-3.

Organic remains from the site yielded both carbonized and uncarbonized material consisting of seeds, wood, leaf fragments and roots. Carbonized seed remains were restricted to culturally related specimens while uncarbonized samples were found in both cultural and noncultural contexts.

Carbonized wood samples contained mostly pine *(Pinus)*, with smaller amounts of poplar/willow *(Populus/Salix)*, maple *(Acer)* and birch *(Betula)*. Carbonized pine was found in hearth samples 17 and 68, and maple in 68.

The presence of carbonized hazelnut, pin cherry, raspberry and elderberry in cultural contexts suggest that if these species were collected by the prehistoric inhabitants, then a summer-fall occupation could be postulated. The low frequency of these remains suggests casual rather than intensive use, and poor organic preservation.

Chronologically, the botanical remains from the site are consistent with the assumption that the occupation of the Foxie Otter site occurred within the last 7,000 years. This conclusion loosely confirms that the Archaic component is no older than the white pine maximum, as spruce is lacking in the botanical remains. Beyond this conclusion, however, the archaeobotanical analysis allowed no discrimination between cultural horizons within the last 7,000 years.

## The Features

Thirteen features were found, consisting of pits, earthen and stone hearths, defined scatters of fire-cracked rock, random fire-cracked rock, and lithic clusters. Each feature was considered in terms of its physical structure, botanical remains and carbon dates. From this, generalizations were made concerning the existence of activity areas. Six of the features are illustrated in the report to demonstrate the variability present.

The features are grouped by site area, A through E. Area A lies along the path to the Scaler's Camp dock (see Fig. 3). Feature 3 is located in square E-0 (not illustrated). It consists of two closely associated concentrations of fire-cracked rock filled with blackened soil and flecks of charcoal. Square E-0 has slumped due to wave action, eroding the earth from beneath the square causing the edges of the two concentrations to fold together. Feature segment 3a extends from the conjunction of quadrants 1, 2, 3 and 4 into quadrant 4. It contains two small retouched scrapers and several chert and vein quartz flakes. A flotation sample taken from 3a yielded carbonized seeds of *Rubus*, *Corylus*, and unknown plants (see Appendix 2). The second part of the feature, 3b, is located on the east wall of quadrant 4. The cultural assemblage in 3b yielded two thin grit-tempered body sherds and several quartz flakes. Flotation analysis indicated traces of *Pinus* and undefined conifer. A single carbon date from feature 3b produced a date of $610 \pm 80$ B.P. (SFU-154) or approximately A.D. 1340. The association of the ceramic sherds and the date are appropriate in their context. Both of the segments of feature 3 give the appearance of being hearths, though the absence of carbonized wood in segment 3a casts doubt that both segments were hearth remains. The cultural material within the structure of the feature attests to its human origin. The association of the ceramic sherd and the carbon sample from segment 3b indicate a Late Woodland origin for the feature.

Excavation of area B provided 4 of the 13 features recorded. These are discussed from north to south.

Feature 4 is located in quadrants 1 and 4 of square 1N0E and in quadrant 3 of square 0N0E (not illustrated). It consists of a 40 cm long lens of charcoal sealed from the base of the humus by a .5 cm thick layer of podzol. Square 1N0E contained scattered fire-cracked rock along the south and east side of the unit in quadrants 3 and 4. This concentration of fire-cracked rock continued through the baulk between 1N0E and 0N0E. Within the concentration of charcoal, several small quartz retouch flakes were found. Along the edge of the charcoal concentration two chert scrapers were located, one in 1N0E and the other in 0N0E.

Flotation samples from feature 4 collected in 1N0E, quadrant 4, level 2, yielded carbonized *Prunus* seed and traces of *Populus/Salix*, *Pinus* and indeterminable porous and conifer charcoal. A second flotation sample was recovered from 1N0E, quadrant 1, level 2, near the edge of feature 4. This sample yielded an unknown carbonized seed, carbonized wood fragments of *Populus/Salix* and *Pinus*, indeterminable diffuse porous hardwood and indeterminable conifer. Three C-14 samples were processed from this feature (SFU-151, -153, -155). SFU-151 yielded a date of $690 \pm 180$ B.P., or approximately A.D. 1260. SFU-153 produced a date of $370 \pm 90$ B.P., or A.D. 1580. Finally, SFU-155 was dated at $1450 \pm 250$ B.P., or A.D. 500. Carbon dates SFU-151 and -153 are statistically comparable. Sample 155 is a statistically different date and may indicate the blending of multiple occupations. Feature 4 has been interpreted as a hearth within an activity area where organic remains may have been prepared during the Late Woodland period.

Feature 5 has two overlapping concentrations of charcoal and fire-cracked rock. Feature 5a (Fig. 4) is a concentration of charcoal surrounded by scattered fire-cracked rock from quadrants 3 and 4 of square 2N0E. The charcoal in this part of the feature was mixed with blackened soil and debris from the humus layer immediately over the feature. Segment 5b is a smaller overlapping concentration of burnt soil at the base of the podzol layer. It extends into the top of the B horizon (see Fig. 5). Quartz and chert flakes were found in close proximity but not within the feature. A flotation sample from feature 5 produced an unknown carbonized seed, carbonized *Pinus* and indeterminable porous conifer charcoal. Feature 5 has no C-14 date associated with it. The feature can be interpreted as a hearth that was utilized during plant preparation in the summer and fall. As neither diagnostic artifacts nor carbon samples were obtained from this feature, a date is not available. It is reasonable to infer, given the proximity to feature 4, that feature 5 dates to the Woodland period.

Feature 12 is located in square 7N0E, quadrant 3, level 2 (Fig. 6). The feature consists of blackened soil and fragments of fire-cracked rock scattered in quadrants 1, 2, 3, and 4 (see Fig. 7). There was a great deal of fragmentary bone in quadrant 2. Numerous quartz and chert flakes were scattered throughout the feature. A scraper was located on the southern periphery of the feature. A flotation sample yielded a carbonized *Sambucus* (elderberry) seed, *Pinus*, and indeterminable porous conifer charcoal fragments. Feature 12 is a possible hearth. It is associated with processing floral and faunal material and with debitage from refitting of stone tools. No C-14 samples were recovered from feature 12. Given the two side-notched Transitional Woodland projectile points recovered from 8N0E and the C-14 date of nearby feature 4, it seems reasonable to infer a Woodland association for feature 12.

Feature 13 is located in 8N0E, quadrant 3, level 2 (Figs. 8 and 9, floor plan and profile respectively). The feature consists of a semicircle of fist-size rock (10–15 cm) enclosing a diffuse scatter of charcoal. Quartz and chert flakes were recovered both within and near the feature. A flotation sample

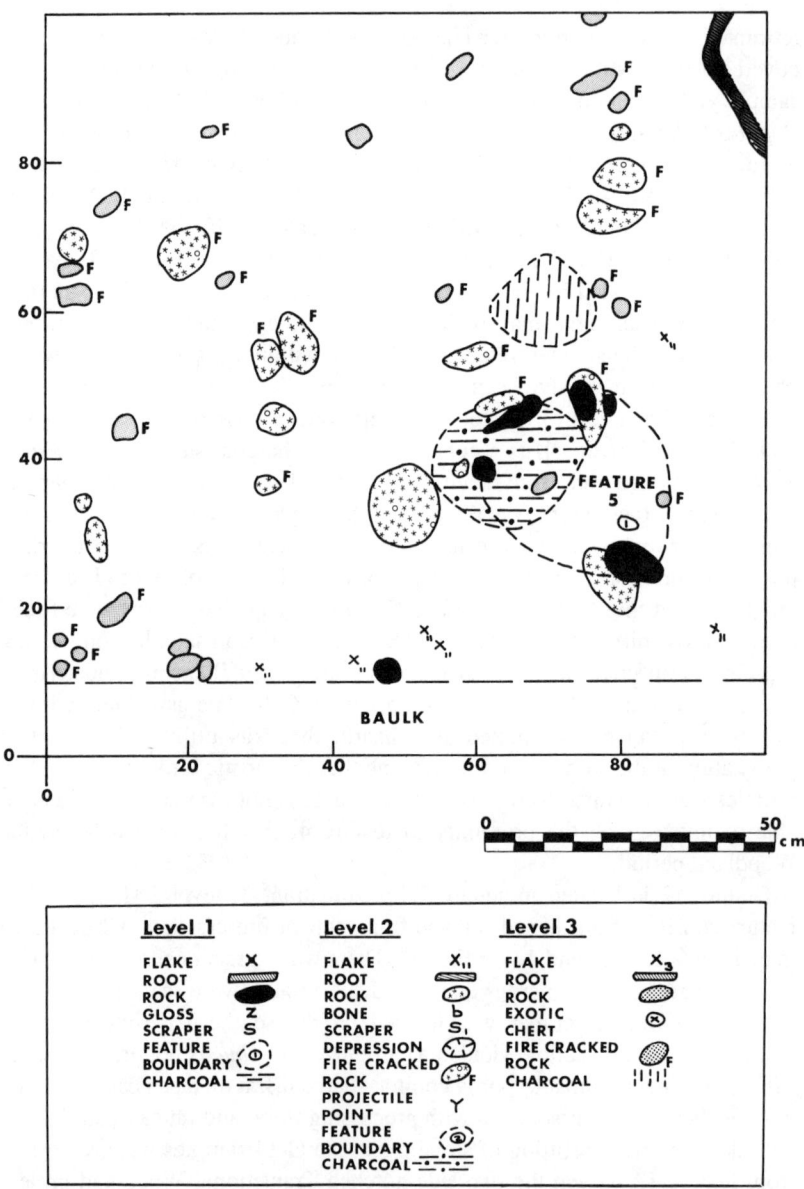

Figure 4. Floor plan of ScE 1N0E.

## Analysis of CdHk-3

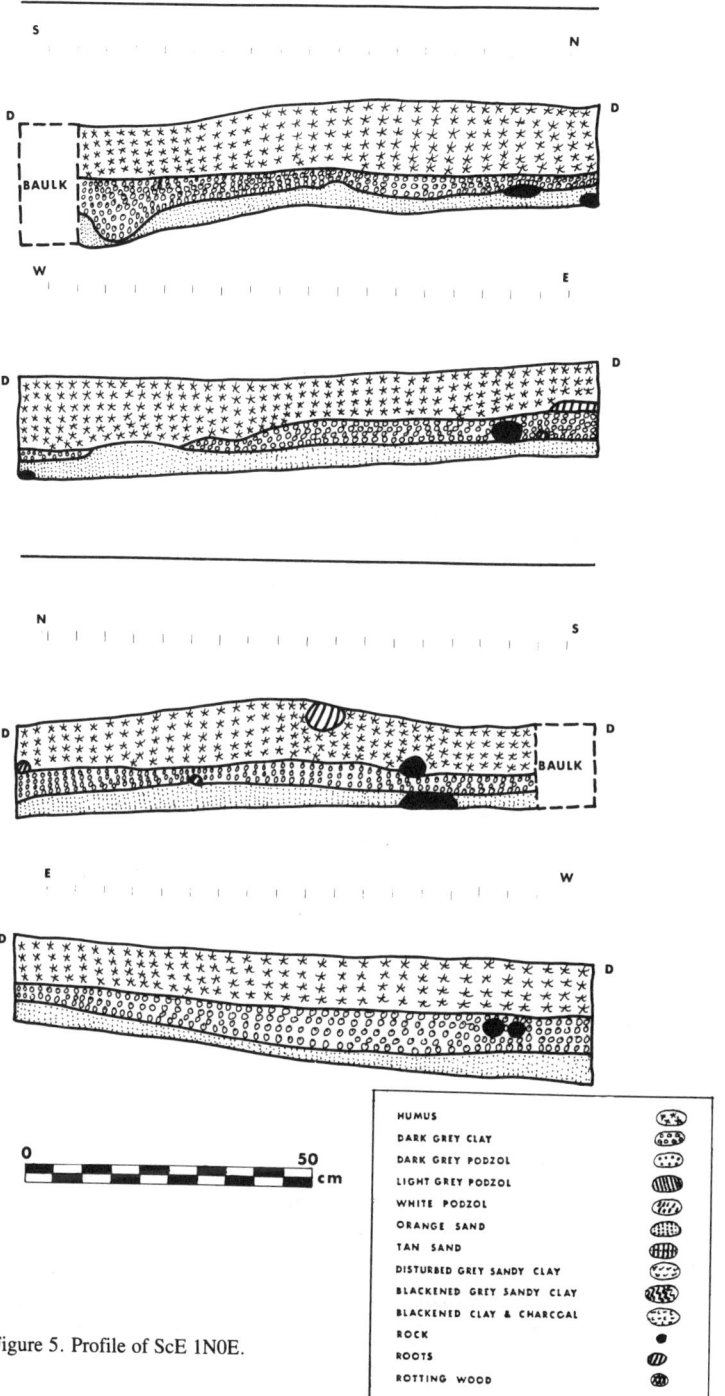

Figure 5. Profile of ScE 1N0E.

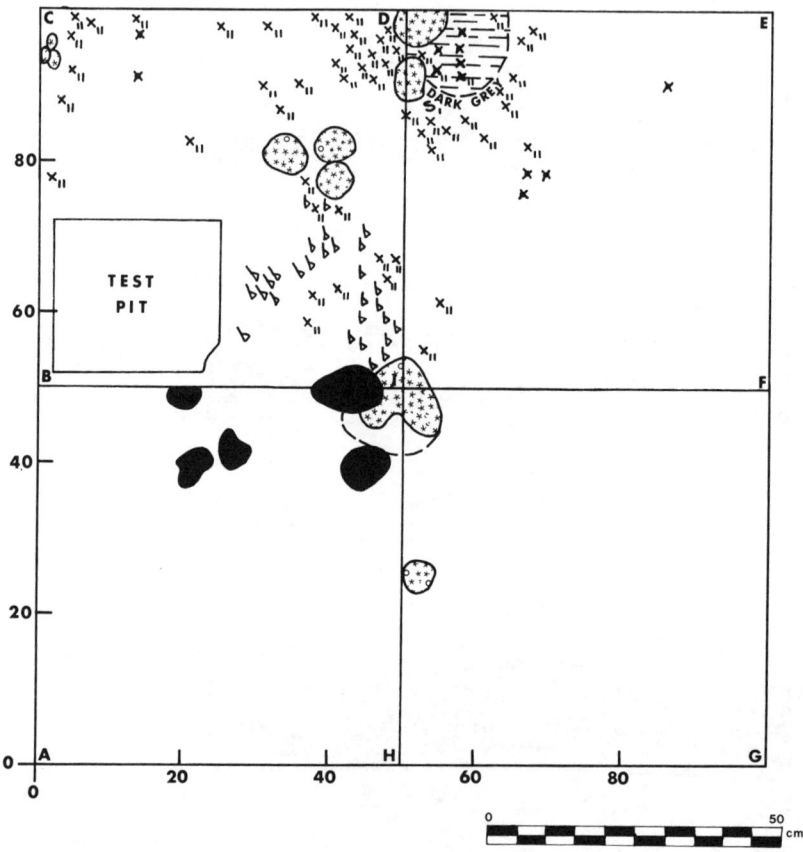

Figure 6. Floor plan of ScE 7N0E. Legend on page 30.

removed from the feature contains a carbonized *Prunus* seed, *Acer*, *Pinus*, and indeterminable conifer charcoal. As with feature 12, the proximity to the Transitional side-notched points in 8N0E implies a Woodland origin. There were no carbon samples processed from this feature.

Next are features 1 and 2, from unit B-0 in site area C, beside the old Moose Run cabin (not illustrated). Feature 1 is in quadrant 3, level 2. It is a 21-cm-deep depression in the podzol immediately at the base of the organic level. In the bottom of the humus, a glass seed bead was found. Though the bead was on top of the feature, it is uncertain if it was associated with the

Analysis of CdHk-3

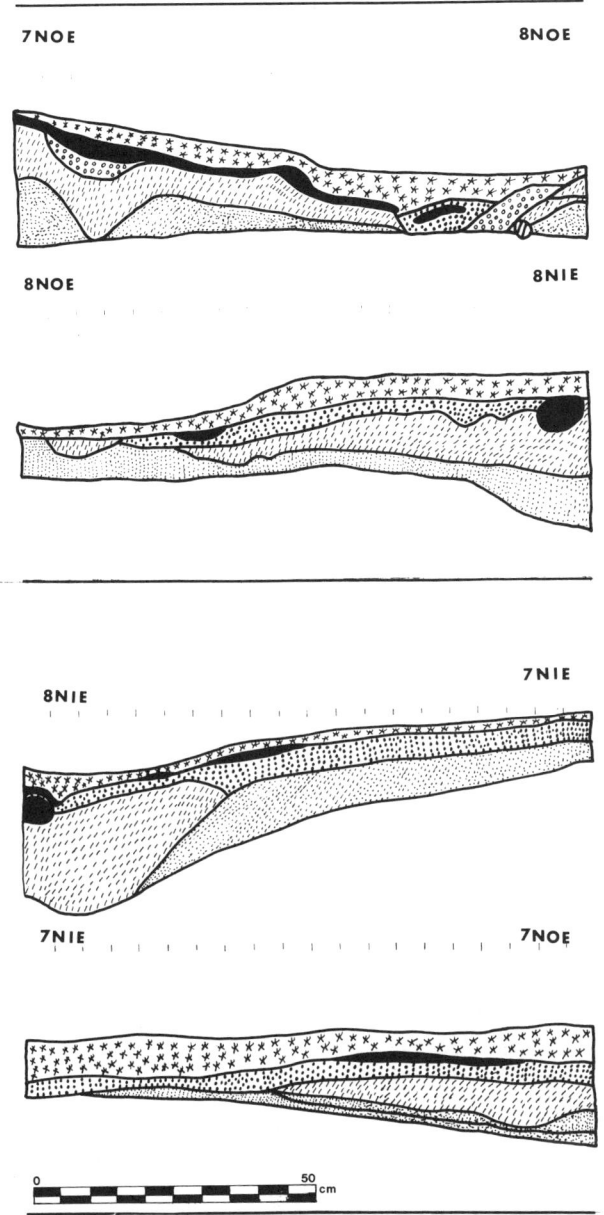

Figure 7. Profile of ScE 7N0E. Legend on page 31.

*34*  *Foxie Otter Site*

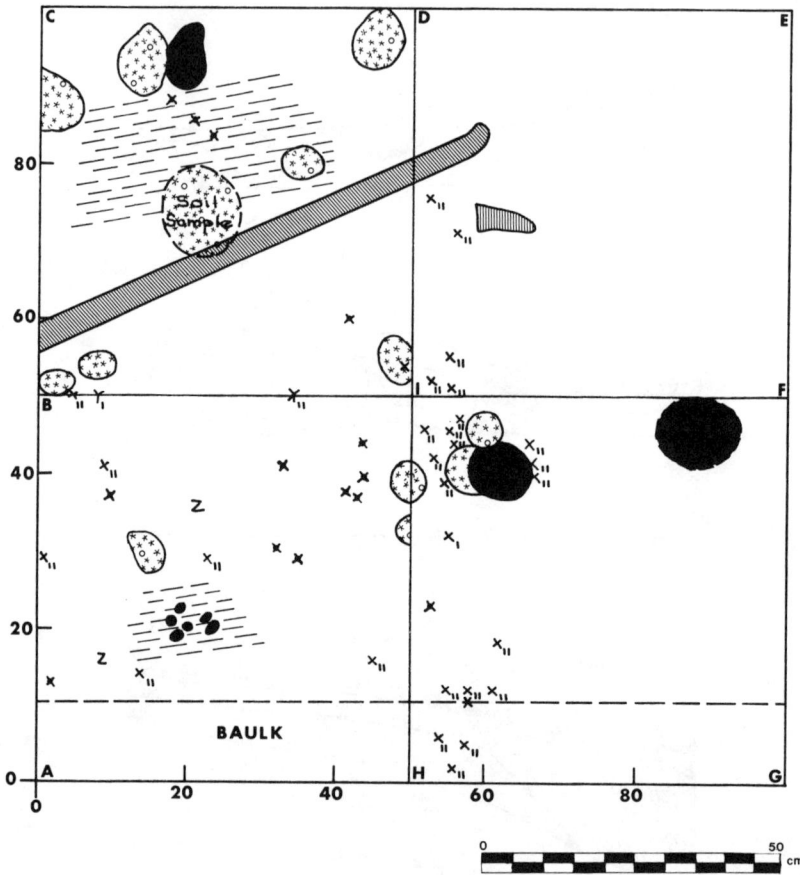

Figure 8. Floor plan of ScE 8N0E. Legend on page 30.

feature. At the base of the pit was a moose calcaneus underlain by fist-sized rocks (10–15 cm) that show no evidence of fire cracking. A flotation sample from the base of the feature yielded a carbonized *Corylus* (hazelnut) seed fragment. Though a C-14 sample was collected, it has not yet been processed.

Feature 2 is located in quadrant 1 near the base of the podzol. It is 2–3 cm below the base of feature 1. The feature consists of a 20 cm crescent-shaped dike of B horizon soil filled with black organic matter. The feature

*Analysis of CdHk-3*

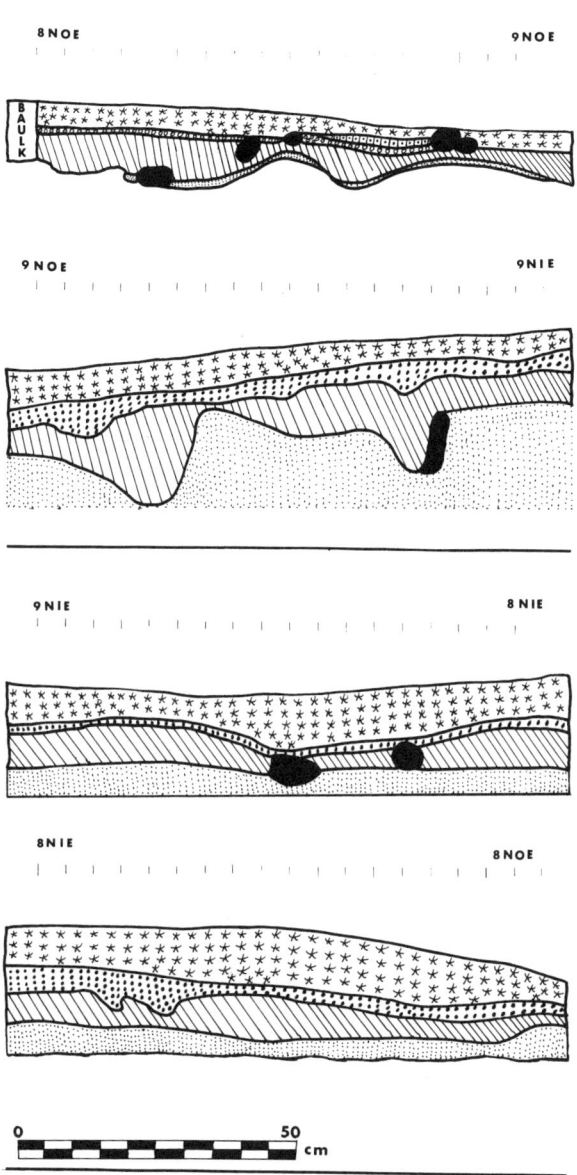

Figure 9. Profile of ScE 8N0E. Legend on page 31.

rests on top of the grey podzol. A C-14 sample was collected, but has not been processed. There was no cultural material found in association with feature 2.

Area D is located along the 38° baseline adjacent to the shoreline of Fox Lake. The excavation of ten one-meter-square units and two half-meter squares yielded one modern and three prehistoric features. A diffuse scatter of debitage and red ochre was found in units 9N2W, 10N2W and 10N3W (called feature 10 at the time of excavation). Feature D (from the 1980 survey) located in quadrant 2 of 10N2W (Fig. 14, profile) is in proximity to the numerous graywacke flakes and flecks of red ochre found in the surrounding podzol horizon. Feature D was a pit which extended from the base of the podzol (level 2) into the B horizon (level 3). It contained a mixture of burnt soil, charcoal and podzol. Several graywacke flakes in the pit were found in context with a charcoal mass that was dated at $7670 \pm 120$ B.P. (I-11,700). Despite the sound integrity of this feature, it must be acknowledged that the area surrounding it has been severely disturbed in recent times. A few years ago, a cottage was dragged up the bank stripping off most of the overburden and disrupting this sector. Fortunately, square 10N2W is in a slight depression and was thus spared being scoured. So far feature D has provided the only Early Archaic date from CdHk-3.

Flotation samples from the feature were lost in the mail on their way to the Royal Ontario Museum for treatment in 1980.

Three other features were found in associated with a dense concentration of graywacke debitage in quadrants 1, 2, 3 and 4 of 14N0W and in the baulks between 14N0W, 14N1W and 15N0W (see Figs. 10–14). Feature 6 was in quadrant 1 of 14N0W. It consisted of a thin lens of burnt soil and charcoal at the edge of a large concentration of graywacke flakes. The lens was sealed from the humus by one to two centimeters of grey podzol. As several graywacke flakes were found in the feature, it was hoped at the time of excavation that a second date on the Archaic component would be possible. Flotation samples taken from this feature yielded no carbonized organic remains. A small charcoal sample from the feature produced a problematic date of $1320 \pm 700$ B.P. (SFU-170). This was subsequently rejected because the lab suspected the sample might have been contaminated. The excavation notes indicate the feature was heavily disturbed by root activity. This may account for some of the contamination of the carbon sample. As a result, feature 6 must be virtually discounted from the analysis.

Feature 11 is located in unit 38°14N1W, quadrant 3, level 2. It consists of a concentration of fire-cracked rock at the edge of the lithic concentration which extends into the square from 14N0W. The rocks were surrounded by burnt soil and flecks of charcoal (Fig. 10). A flotation sample taken from the feature revealed the presence of carbonized *Sambucus* (elderberry) seed fragments and indeterminate conifer charcoal. It was not possible, however, to

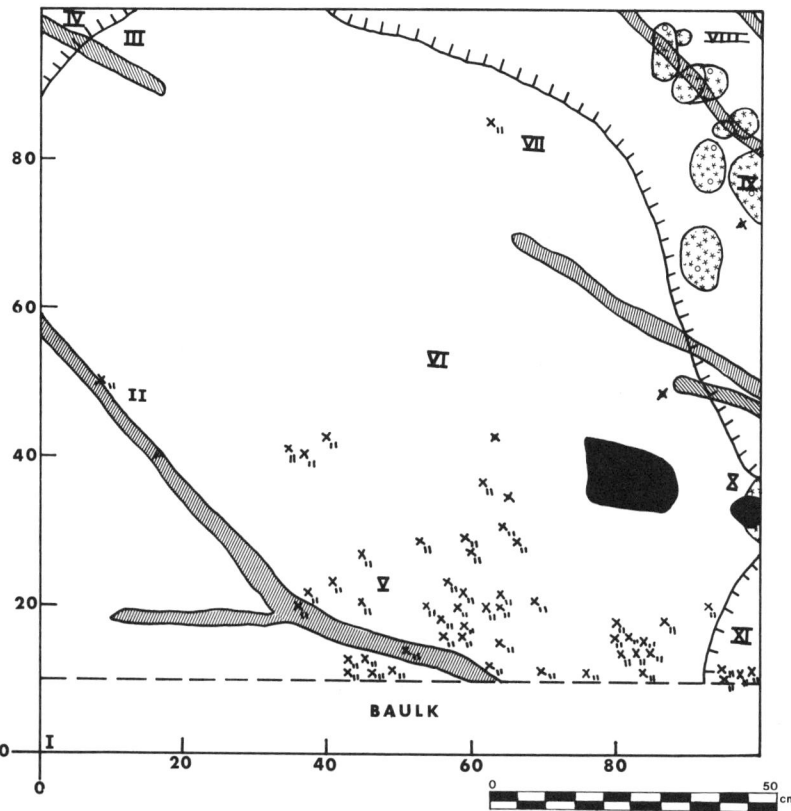

Figure 10. Floor plan of 38°14N1W. Legend on page 30.

collect enough charcoal to date this feature. Based upon the structure of the feature and the results of the flotation analysis, it is reasonable to assume that feature 11 is the disturbed remains of a prehistoric hearth. It appears that the feature is associated with the activities which produced the lithic scatter borders.

Feature 8 is located in unit 15N0W, quadrant 1, levels 1 through 3. It is a modern fire pit containing bits of glass, the base of a 12-gauge paper case shotgun shell and charcoal. Unfortunately, this disturbance cuts into the

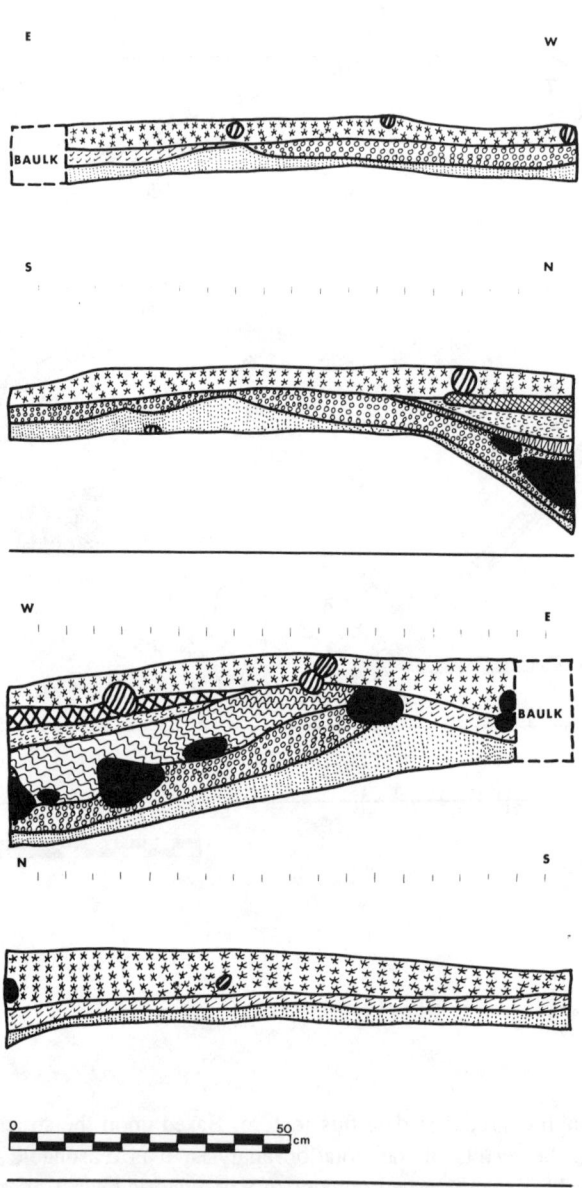

Figure 11. Profile of 38°14N1W. Legend on page 31.

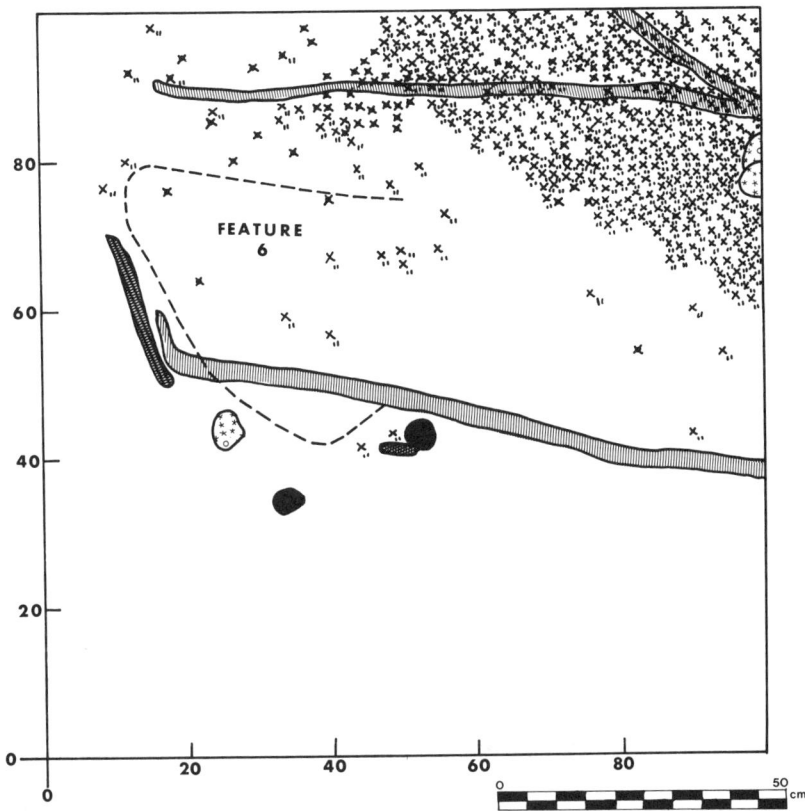

Figure 12. Floor plan of 38°14N0W. Legend on page 30.

northern extension of the graywacke scatter concentrated in 14N0W. In addition to this recent feature, 15N0W is heavily disturbed by root mat.

Moving to site area E on Otter Slide Island, feature 7 is in unit 1N0W, quadrant 3, level 3. The feature intrudes 30 cm into the northeast corner of the unit. A significant portion of the feature lies outside the square. It consists of pieces of fire-cracked rock mixed with burnt soil, bits of charcoal and chert flakes. A flotation sample removed from the top of the sample lacked any plant remains, casting doubt upon the nature of the feature. It had been originally presumed a hearth. It was not possible to collect enough charcoal

*40*  *Foxie Otter Site*

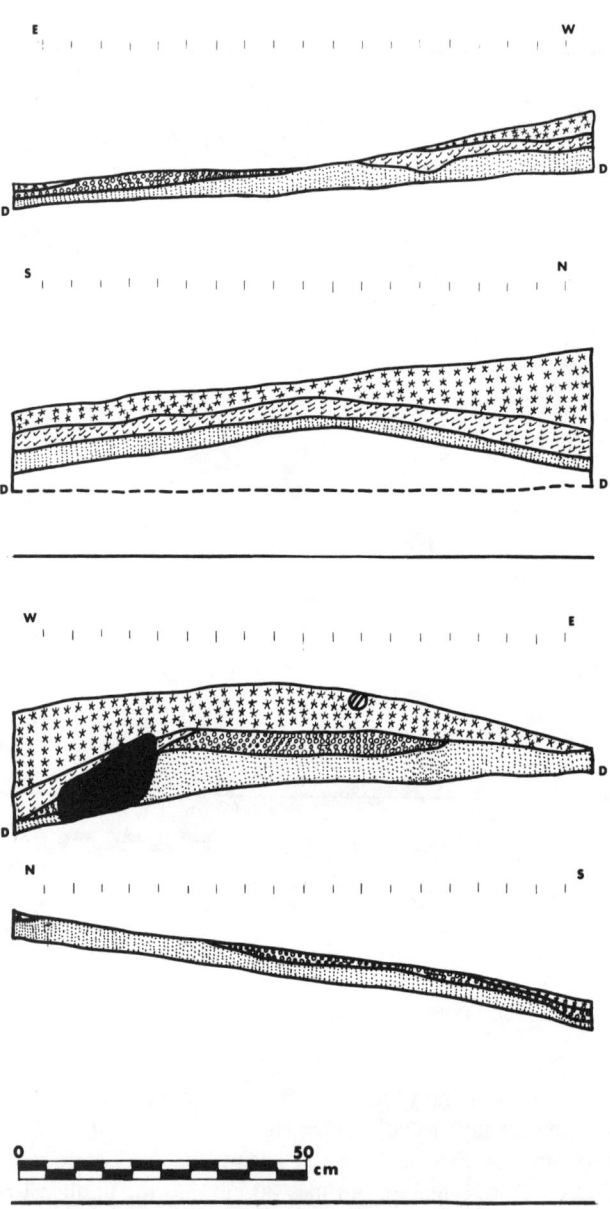

Figure 13. Profile of 38°14N0W. Legend on page 31.

# Analysis of CdHk-3

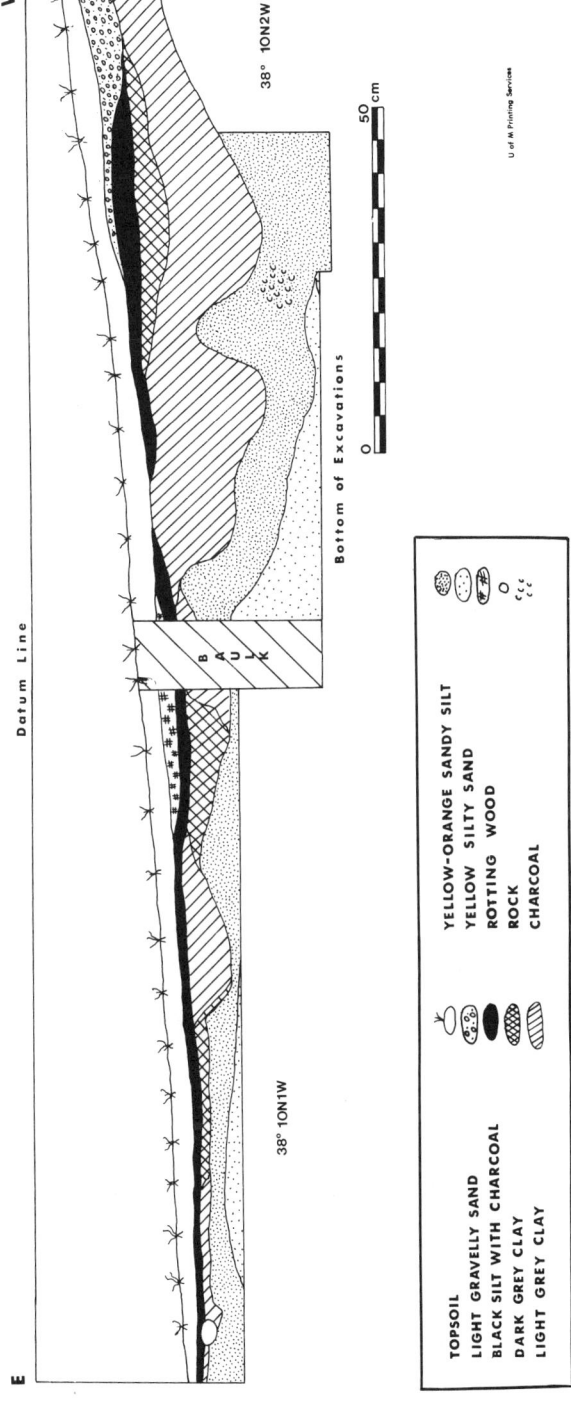

Figure 14. Profile of south wall, 38°10N1W.

flecks from the hearth to date the feature. A carbon sample was collected from a charcoal lens in quadrant 1, level 2. Unfortunately, the lens was not in direct association with feature 7. The date of 1840 ± 350 B.P. (SFU-171) may well date a forest fire.

The majority of the features at the Foxie Otter site were the remnants of hearths. Scattered organic and lithic remains found in association with them may indicate generalized occupation areas. The predominance of hearth, pit and rock scatters is typical of features found on sites in the northern forest. In the absence of other evidence, the presence of a hearth and scattered fire-cracked rock may be indicative of a dwelling (Binford and Quimby 1972:352). As post molds are absent at the Foxie Otter site, hearths and fire-cracked rock are our best clue to the location of probable house structures. The six units excavated in area B appear to have cut through segments of several activity areas that may have been house structures.

## Lithic Analysis

With the exception of the two sherds of grit-tempered pottery and a single seed bead, the cultural assemblage from CdHk-3 is composed of lithic tools and debitage. Consequently, primary artifactual analysis will focus on the lithic remains.

Lithic assemblages consist of two broad subtypes, tools and debitage, both of which will be considered in this analysis. In this study, the term *tool* is used to mean any worked piece of stone for which there is some evidence of use. The term *debitage* is used morphologically to describe all products of the reduction process.[5] A discussion of the nature of lithic finds on the site precedes interpretation of the data.

Lithic remains were located in three different contexts at Foxie Otter: (1) as random finds not associated with other cultural features, (2) in concentrations of lithic material, and (3) in concentrations associated with nonlithic cultural features (e.g., a hearth). These criteria are valid for both surface and excavated remains at CdHk-3.

As lithic material is the most common type of artifact type in many northern sites, its presence was used as the principal cultural indicator during site survey. Consequently there may have been a bias against cultural features that lacked lithic evidence. Binford (1972:180) states that "areas in which activities resulted in the loss or abandonment of the greatest number of items is not necessarily the same area where the greatest concentration of features

---

[5]In Appendix 4 where the residue analysis of 40 tools and and 45 pieces of debitage is discussed in detail, the word "flakage" is used, rather than debitage, since residue analysis of the debitage shows that many of the debitage flakes were used as tools.

occurred." Similarly Janes (1983) observed among the modern Dene that discarded material is very frequently cleared away from activity areas. By analogy it is reasonable to assume that debris such as flakes may frequently have been cleared away from central activity areas like a hearth.

The use of stone tools as an indicator of prehistoric occupation tends to restrict the amount of cultural variability represented in the test sample. If a randomizing factor is not introduced into the inner site sampling procedure, a bias toward lithic activity areas may potentially result.

Some observations regarding the distribution of lithic and nonlithic features at CdHk-3 can be made. Of the ten hearth features recorded, seven hearths had scattered stone tools and flakes in association. One hearth contained no lithic material. The remaining two hearths were near dense lithic scatters. Conversely, only one dense concentration of flakes was not found in direct association with a hearth feature. That concentration was embedded within a diffuse scatter of fire-cracked rock that was part of an occupation area extending from a hearth in the next unit. Following Binford (1972:180), the assumption has been made that the concentration might be within part of a house structure. In the majority of excavated squares, lithic material occurred in diffuse arrangements, frequently in association with hearths. These features reflect generalized activity areas that were transformed continually by successive activities (Stevenson 1985:5). When lithic debitage was found in dense, nonrandom concentrations, either a specialized lithic activity area or a lack of pre-abandonment cleaning of a more generalized feature is implied.

Despite the small total number of features excavated (12), there are a few observations that can be made. First, Binford's (1972) and Janes's (1983) observation—that features do not necessarily occur in areas of highest artifact concentration—is not evident in the sample from CdHk-3, as seven of the ten hearths were in association with concentrations of lithic material. This is supported by the fact that three out of the four dense lithic concentrations were in close association with nonlithic features. Despite the sampling bias toward areas where lithic reduction took place, it may be implied that flint knapping frequently occurred near the fire, and further, that the random occurrence of flakes around hearths may reflect those scattered by subsequent activities or clean up.

In order to examine changes in the technical processes that may have taken place at CdHk-3, the lithic analysis will concentrate on assemblage variability (Fig. 15). To this end, a series of hypotheses were tested to determine if there was significant assemblage variability for tools across the site. As a broad, working hypothesis, it has been assumed that there is no significant degree of variability in lithic tools from one section of the site to another. This was examined in terms of four variables: tool type, weight, lithic material and use. A second working hypothesis assumed no significant degree of

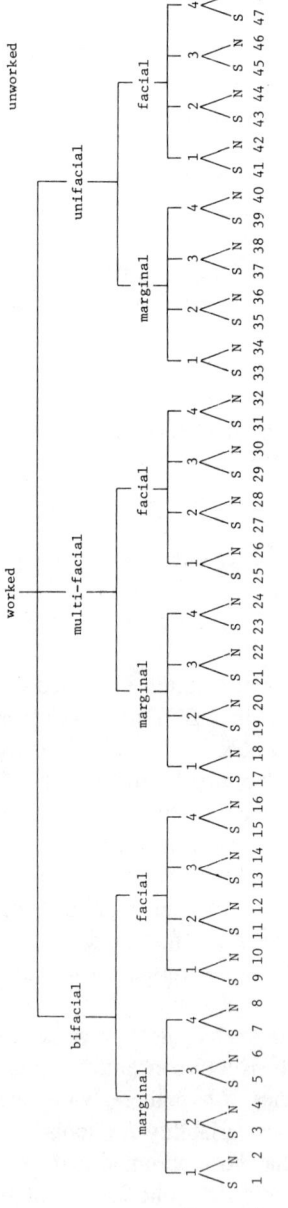

Figure 15. Typing key for lithic tools.

variability in lithic technology across the site as reflected by lithic debitage. Reduction variability was expressed in terms of flake type, weight, and lithic material. Heat treatment was also recorded, but the reliability of visually isolating heat altered specimens across four different raw materials is difficult. Also, when lithic production is being undertaken in hearth areas, it may be hard to differentiate intentional from accidental altering (Rick 1978:4).

Tool and debitage types are based upon a series of technological attributes that are designed to produce inclusive sets or types. Tools were defined by the following criteria: (1) was the piece worked, (2) was it bifacial, multifacial or unifacially flaked, (3) were the edges predominantly marginal or facially flaked, (4) how many edges were worked, and (5) were the edges steep or shallow (i.e., less or greater than 45 degrees). These criteria are fairly straightforward with the exception of edge angle. Instead of recording the precise edge angle, David Pokotylo suggested that his experimental data indicated that the two-category system would reflect significant variability while simplifying the analysis (1981, personal communication). The combination of these variables can be combined to produce 48 possible types of tools (see Fig. 15).

When the 43 tools from CdHk-3 were analyzed, 17 different types were found on the site. There were 8 biface, 2 multiface and 7 unifacial tool types present. Only 4 of the 17 types of tools had four or more worked edges. Nine of the categories present had only one or two worked edges. This may indicate a tendency toward expedient implements as opposed to stylized forms.

By far the most common tool type on the site was type 41, conventionally classed as an end scraper. A distant second was type 10, an expedient biface with one worked edge. The next most frequent types were 13 and 34, a three-edged biface and a uniface respectively, suggesting a nonspecialized preference in the tool forms present at the site. The only stylized artifacts were three projectile points represented by types 15 and 16. Two of the projectile points came from within 5 cm of each other in area B. The context of these two points would seem to indicate they were associated with a single episode. Type 41 was the only tool present in all areas across the site. The tool assemblage would seem to reflect secondary processing (i.e., scraping and cutting) as opposed to faunal procurement or primary butchering. These latter activities might have been reflected by a higher percentage of projectile points and multi-edged bifaces.

Gross tool size was controlled for by the use of tool weight. The decision was made to use a single metric variable because the majority of lithic materials lack forms that could be determined by strict stylistic considerations. For example, of the 43 tools recovered from CdHk-3 (40 of which were analyzed for residue in Appendix 4), most were what Arundale (1980:470) would call expedient tools, created from local materials or small

## TABLE 2
### Summary of Tool Types

| Tool Type | Edge Type | Area Flaked | No. of Edges | Edge Angle |
|---|---|---|---|---|
| 2 | B | M | 1 | N |
| 3 | B | M | 2 | S |
| 9 | B | F | 1 | S |
| 10 | B | F | 1 | N |
| 13 | B | F | 3 | S |
| 14 | B | F | 3 | N |
| 15 | B | F | 4 | S |
| 16 | B | F | 4 | N |
| 19 | M | M | 2 | S |
| 29 | M | F | 3 | S |
| 33 | U | M | 1 | S |
| 34 | U | M | 1 | S |
| 41 | U | F | 2 | N |
| 42 | U | F | 1 | N |
| 43 | U | F | 2 | S |
| 45 | U | F | 3 | S |
| 47 | U | F | 4 | S |

B = biface  
M = multiface  
U = uniface  

M = marginal  
F = facial  

N = narrow (<45°)  
S = steep (>45°)

fragments of imported substances, used and discarded. This contrasts with forms that are stylistic indicators that may be recorded in terms of shape and form (Arundale 1980:471). As a result of these considerations, it was decided to use a single metric variable that could give a rough indication of size without creating patterned forms.

The decision to use weight as the single metric variable was not without problems. Although weight gives a rough indication of size, it is not always a good indicator of process. For instance, Magne (1983) has recently demonstrated that flake weight is not a reliable demonstration of reduction se-

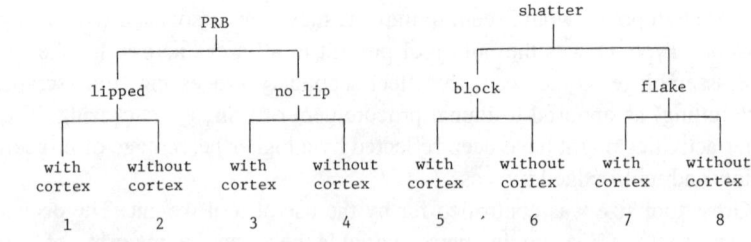

* = numerical type

Figure 16. Typing key for lithic debitage.

Figure 17. Archaic graywacke core tools (38° baseline, surface).
  a. bifacial knife b. bifacial knife

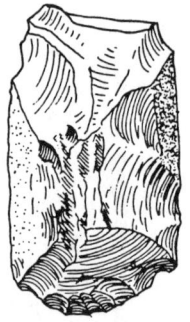

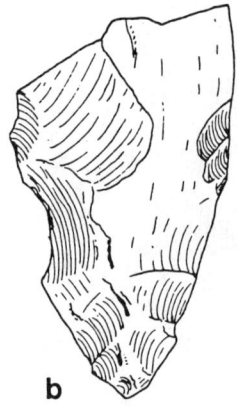
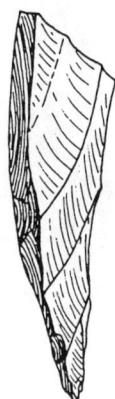
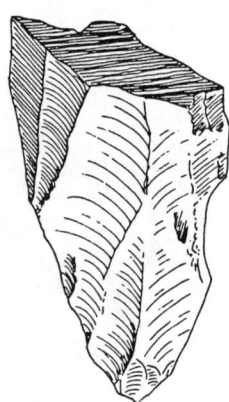

Figure 18. Archaic graywacke core tools (38° baseline, surface).
  a. end scraper b. bifacial knife

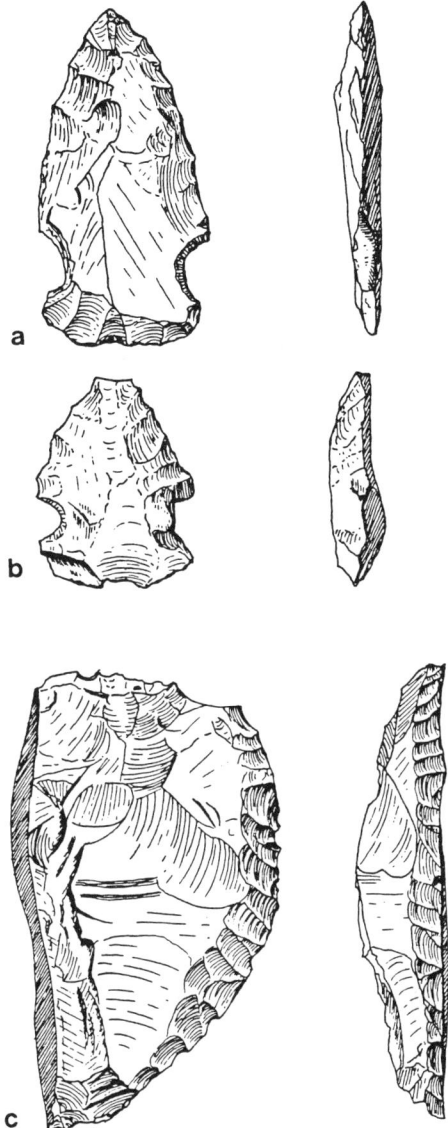

Figure 19. Woodland flake tools (ScE 8W0E).
    a. Transitional Woodland projectile point (chert)
    b. Transitional Woodland projectile point (chert)
    c. Unifacial scraper fragment (chert)

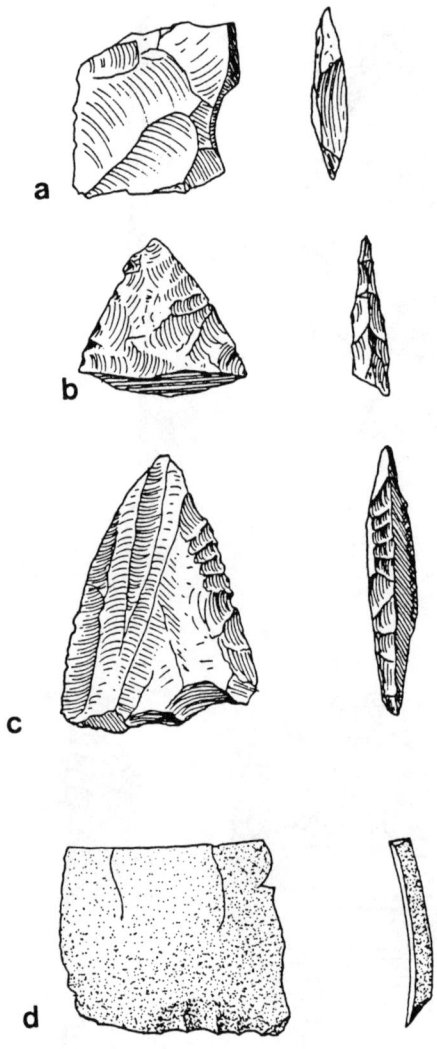

Figure 20. Woodland flake tools from Otter Slide Island.
   a. utilized chert flake (surface)
   b. chert projectile point fragment (surface)
   c. quartz Late Woodland projectile point (0E0S)
   d. chert retouched flake
Scale 2:1

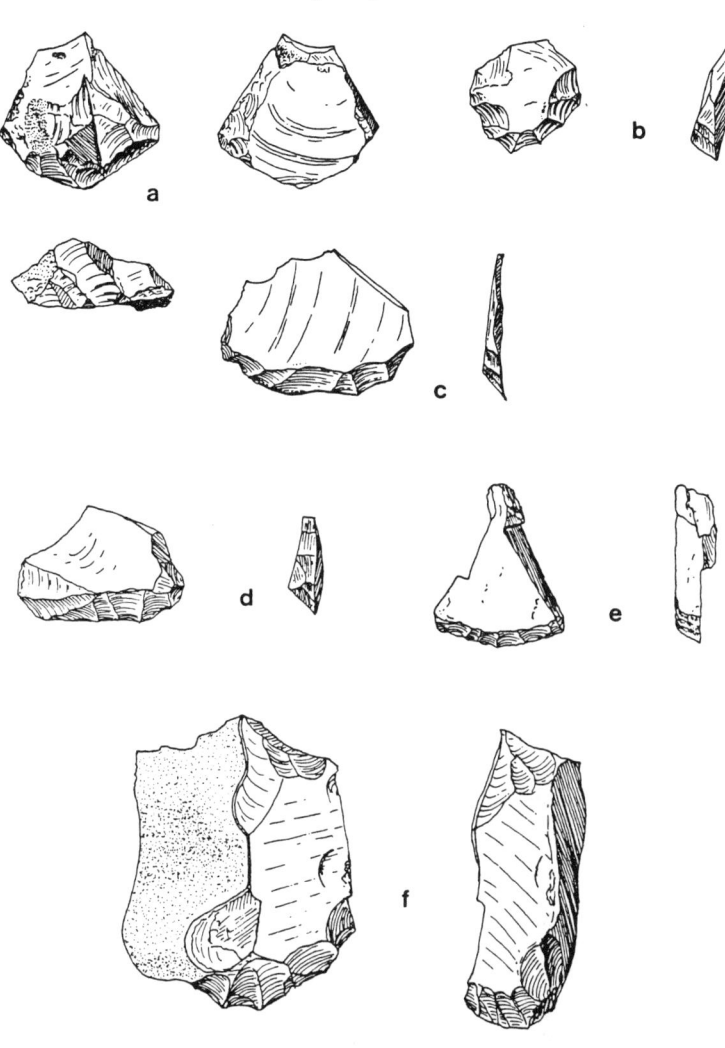

Figure 21. Woodland flake tools (surface 0W0E).
  a. chert end scraper
  b. chert retouched flake
  c. chert retouched flake
  d. chert retouched flake
  e. chert retouched flake
  f. chert end scraper
Scale 2:1

TABLE 3
Percentage of Tool Types Present on CdHk-3

| Tool Type | Area A | Area B | Area C | Area D | Area E | N | % |
|---|---|---|---|---|---|---|---|
| 41 | 4 | 5 | 1 | 1 | 3 | 14 | 33% |
| 10 | 1 | 0 | 0 | 0 | 5 | 6 | 14% |
| 33 | 1 | 1 | 0 | 0 | 0 | 2 | 5% |
| 42 | 1 | 0 | 0 | 0 | 0 | 1 | 2% |
| 47 | 1 | 0 | 0 | 0 | 0 | 1 | 2% |
| 43 | 0 | 2 | 0 | 0 | 0 | 2 | 5% |
| 15 | 0 | 1 | 0 | 0 | 1 | 2 | 5% |
| 11 | 0 | 1 | 0 | 0 | 0 | 2 | 2% |
| 13 | 0 | 0 | 0 | 4 | 0 | 4 | 10% |
| 45 | 0 | 0 | 0 | 1 | 0 | 1 | 2% |
| 02 | 0 | 0 | 0 | 1 | 0 | 1 | 2% |
| 34 | 0 | 0 | 0 | 2 | 2 | 4 | 10% |
| 14 | 0 | 0 | 0 | 0 | 1 | 1 | 2% |
| 19 | 0 | 0 | 0 | 0 | 1 | 1 | 2% |
| 03 | 0 | 0 | 0 | 0 | 1 | 1 | 2% |
| 09 | 0 | 0 | 0 | 0 | 1 | 1 | 2% |
| Total | 8 | 10 | 1 | 9 | 15 | 43 | 100% |
|  | 19% | 23% | 2% | 21% | 35% |  |  |

TABLE 4
A Breakdown of Tool Weight for CdHk-3

WEIGHT
Minimum = .2
Maximum = 104.2
Range = 104
Sum = 590.1
Mean = 13.723
Median = 2.4
Mode = Multi-Modal
Variance = 711.074
Standard Deviation = 26.666
Standard Error of Mean = 4.115
95% Confidence Interval = 5.659 - 21.788
99% Confidence Interval = 3.128 - 24.318

UNBIASED ESTIMATES OF POPULATION
Variance = 728.004
Standard Deviation = 26.982

DATA DISTRIBUTION COEFFICIENTS
Skewness = 2.319
Kurtosis = 4.174

Valid Cases = 43
Missing Cases = 0
Response Percent = 100.0%

## TABLE 5
### Anova of Tool Type, Material and Area

ANOVA SUMMARY TABLE

| Source of Variation | df | Sum of Squares | Mean Squares | F | Significance Level |
|---|---|---|---|---|---|
| Between Groups | 3 | 3095.46 | 1031.82 | 5.43 | 0.002 |
| Within Groups | 168 | 31922.2 | 190.01 | | |
| | 171 | 35017.6 | | | |

GROUP STATISTICS

| Group | N | Missing | Mean | SD |
|---|---|---|---|---|
| SITE AREA | 43 | 0 | 3.3 | 1.6 |
| TOOL TYPE | 43 | 0 | 5.6 | 4.98 |
| WEIGHT | 43 | 0 | 13.72 | 26.98 |
| LITHIC RAW MATERIAL | 43 | 0 | 3.53 | 2.18 |

$t = 3.505$ SITE AREA
$p < .001$ WEIGHT

$t = 2.731$ TOOL TYPE
$p = .006$ WEIGHT

$t = 3.427$ WEIGHT
$p < .001$ LITHIC RAW MATERIAL

## TABLE 6
### Breakdown of Tools by Weight and Site Area

| | Site Area | | | | |
|---|---|---|---|---|---|
| | A | B | C | D | E |
| Mean | 1.6 g | 4.93 g | 0.2 g | 32.667 g | 15.587 g |
| Median | 1.4 g | 2.45 g | 0.2 g | 42 g | 2 g |
| Standard Dev. | .689 | 4.551 | 0 | 29.392 | 33.839 |

## TABLE 7
### Lithic Raw Material Used in Tools by Site Area

| MATERIAL | AREA | | | | | TOTALS | |
|---|---|---|---|---|---|---|---|
| | A | B | C | D | E | N | % |
| Quartz(ite) | 4 | 2 | 0 | 3 | 5 | 14 | 32.5% |
| Chert | 3 | 8 | 1 | 0 | 2 | 14 | 32.5% |
| Greywacke | 0 | 0 | 0 | 6 | 0 | 6 | 14% |
| Burnt chert | 1 | 0 | 0 | 0 | 7 | 8 | 19% |
| Slate | 0 | 0 | 0 | 0 | 1 | 1 | 2% |
| Totals | 8 | 10 | 1 | 9 | 15 | 43 | |
| | 19% | 23% | 2% | 21% | 35% | | |

quence. Magne's experimental data indicate that while "it is only logical that as tools are reduced they become smaller, the same is not necessarily true of debitage" (1983:125). Conversely, Buchner (1981:47) has shown that weight is a successful variable for the separation of tools on the basis of absolute size. Although CdHk-3 has a variety of raw materials as opposed to the single raw material used in Buchner's experiment, weight is still considered a viable measure for remains with amorphous shapes. Preliminary observations led to the assumption that specific assemblages are separable on the basis of size as controlled by weight.

Tool size across the site is highly variable. This difference is particularly obvious in the grouping of areas A, B, C and E where the median tool weight is below 3 grams and area D with a median of 42 grams. The median was chosen over the mean because of extreme outlying weights which affected the latter measurement. With the exception of several randomly retouched chert flakes, the tool assemblage from area D consists of large graywacke bifaces and an end scraper. These tools have been linked through debitage with a feature dated to the Early Archaic. The chert and quartz tools in the other areas are associated with Woodland contexts. The distribution in area D is skewed by the presence of three retouched flake scrapers made of chert. These implements were present in the podzol near the south end of the 38 degree baseline well away from the graywacke concentration. As a result, the standard deviation of artifacts for area D is much larger than would have been expected if only the graywacke artifacts had been present.

The standard deviation of artifacts in area E, on the other hand, reflects a diverse tool assemblage present in the mixed surface collection. While area D is interpreted as having two discrete assemblages, area E reflects a more heterogeneous composition that may or may not be indicative of multiple episodes of occupation. Based upon this preliminary examination of the variable weight, it can be postulated that size, as reflected by weight, is a significant variable for intrasite comparisons.

The third category considered is material. Material was chosen as a variable because on an intuitive level it demonstrates variability between areas within the site. Some components lack significant quantities of locally available graywacke (A, B, C and E), but contain chert and quartz. In area D, the reverse is true.

As with weight, this separation is most evident between the proposed Archaic section of the site and the Woodland components. From these observations it can be postulated that material is a significant variable on an intra-area basis. If material is shown to vary significantly across the site, it will be an important element in defining assemblage variability.

## Residue Analysis

The last factor analyzed was tool use. In this study, chemical tests were used to determine if residues were present on the surfaces of tools and debitage. The identification of residues on lithic remains was used as a basis for predicting tool function and activity areas. Residue analysis was chosen over macro-edge (Tringham et al. 1974) or micro-abrasion and polish (Keeley 1980) use-wear analysis for Fox Lake, as it offered a more precise view of function.

Forty tools recovered from CdHk-3 were subjected to residue analysis in a blind test by Michael Broderick. At the time Broderick undertook the tests, he knew only that the site came from northern Ontario and that one of the components might date to around 7000 B.P. The results of these tests and a more complete explanation of methodology can be found in Appendix 4.

Broderick made use of three chemical spot tests to determine if blood, starch, fat or resin were present on the tool surface. The chemical reagents used for the spot tests in this analysis were: benzidine (4–4' diamino biphenyl) to test for the presence of blood; Sudan III (tetrazobenzine-B-naphthol) to detect fat and resin; and potassium iodide (KI) to test for starch. Broderick's working hypothesis was that blood and fat on a tool imply that it was used on animal tissue; starch implies use on plant tissue; and resin suggests either use on wood or that a hafting agent was present. If fat is present and blood is absent on a specimen, Broderick's experiments led him to hypothesize that the object was used on cooked meat. All three tests are relatively common chemical diagnostic methods. Their application in archaeology is very promising, but care is required as they have not as yet been adequately proven experimentally in an archaeological context. Thus, though interesting, the results should not be accepted uncritically.

Residue analysis was performed to examine the assumption that artifact types reflect functional categories. Broadly stated, the research hypothesis maintains that tools of the same physical type as defined in Figure 15 will contain similar residues. The greater the number of residue combinations on a tool, the more general was its use.

Before examining Broderick's conclusions, it is necessary to consider artifacts which contain no residues. A lack of residue indicates one of three possibilities: (1) the object was not a tool; (2) the tool has been fired since use (see Appendix 4); and (3) the tool was new at the time of abandonment and had not been used. In the present study, it is not possible to determine which of these factors is responsible for the absence of residue. Tools with no residues will not be considered within the parameters of the use analysis.

Of the 40 tools tested from CdHk-3, 27 contained traces of residues while 13 were barren of residues. Within the group that had residues, two contained

TABLE 8
Tool Use Residue Analysis

| | |
|---|---|
| Tools Tested | N = 40 |
| Residue Present | N = 27 |
| Residue Absent | N = 13 |

Percentage Breakdown of Tools with Residue

| Animal | Plant | Both | Hafting | Total |
|---|---|---|---|---|
| 59% | 15% | 18.5% | 7.5% | 100.0% |

TABLE 9
Residues by Tool Type

| | | RESIDUE | | | |
|---|---|---|---|---|---|
| Art.# | Tool Type | Blood | Fat | Starch | Resin |
| 34 | 41 | X | X | X | X |
| 75 | 2 | X* | X* | | X* |
| 134 | 41 | X | X | | |
| 149 | 41 | X | X | | |
| 156 | 42 | X | X | | |
| 163 | 10 | X* | X* | | X* |
| 164 | 34 | | | | X |
| 171 | 45 | | | | X |
| 172 | 13 | | | | X |
| 173 | 13 | X | X | | X |
| 180 | 13 | X | X | X | |
| 184 | 19 | X | X | | |
| 186 | 14 | | X | | X |
| 189 | 41 | X | X | X | |
| 199 | 43 | | X* | | X* |
| 208 | 13 | X | X | | X |
| 355 | 41 | | | X* | X* |
| 396 | 33 | | X* | | X* |
| 419 | 10 | X | X | | |
| 423 | 41 | | X | | |
| 463 | 15 | | | | X* |
| 464 | 16 | X* | X* | | X* |
| 477 | 43 | | X | | X |
| 4253 | 15 | X | X | | |
| 4271 | 41 | | | | X* |
| 4278 | 10 | X | | | |
| 4279 | 10 | X | X | | |

\* = hafted tool

only fat. Broderick infers this as evidence of use on cooked meat. Seven artifacts revealed traces of both fat and blood. From this it is postulated that the implements were used on either raw meat and/or hides. Two tools contained traces of blood, fat and starch. The blending of these three items would suggest that the tools were used on both plant and animal remains. Three tools contained resin along the working edges. Broderick speculated that these were wood-working implements. The two projectile points tested contained resin around the notches. From this, hafting was predicted. As resin was the only residue on the points, it may be inferred that these tools had either been made or refitted shortly before their deposition at the site. Two other tools revealed traces of blood, fat and resin. As the resin was on their cutting/scraping edges it is reasonable to assume that they were used on both plant and animal tissues. By contrast, on two other implements which contained blood, fat and resin the location of the resin around the proximal end indicated the presence of hafting. Another contained a mix of starch and resin around the basal end implying that a handle had been bound to the tool. Finally, one artifact had all the residues present in a collage which seems to indicate a very general use (Table 9).

Of the 27 tools which contained residues, 59% were used on animal tissue. Within that subset, six were believed to have been utilized on cooked meat. The next largest category (18%) contains implements used on both plant and animal tissue. Slightly less frequent are items restricted to plant tissues alone (15%). Finally 7% of the sample, shows only evidence of hafting.

Broderick maintains that because 32% of the sample does not contain residues, tools were being made and/or refitted on the site. The high frequency of use on animal tissue indicates the importance of butchering, hide processing and food preparation at CdHk-3. Last, of the tools used only on plant tissue three of four had resin as opposed to starch. Broderick interprets this as evidence of wood-working. The pattern which emerges from the residue analysis is the predominance of generalized use, which the tools exhibit. There is no significant change in this pattern over time from the Archaic to the Woodland periods. The tool assemblage is dominated by expedient implements used for a variety of applications. Perhaps the most interesting observation is in the Early Archaic assemblage, where the large core tools that in most instances would be called preforms have in fact been heavily utilized both on wood and for the preparation of meat. This calls into question the indiscriminate use of the term preform for the large biface cores so often associated with Archaic and quarry sites in the upper Great Lakes. The other slightly surprising discovery is that two of the three projectile points found on the site show no evidence of blood residues. This implies that they were either newly produced or had been heat treated to ease refitting after their last use. Hunting or procurement is far less evident at this site than the processing of both plant and animal materials.

These insights are possible because of residue analysis. Given the coarse grain of the quartz, quartzite, and graywacke which predominate much of the collection, more traditional use-wear analysis simply would not have been able to produce this level of detail.

## Research Hypotheses for Lithic Tools

Ten hypotheses were formed proposing relationships between tool weight, material, residue and area. The first hypothesis tested was a proposed relationship between tool weight and tool type. The independent variable type was compared to the dependent variable weight in a one-way Analysis of Variance (Anova). That test yielded a between-group $F$ score of 2.569, which with 16 degrees of freedom is significant at the 0.01 level. This score indicates that weight is a significant factor affecting variability for artifact type in the overall tool assemblage.

A second measure of association, *Eta*, was used to determine how dissimilar the means of the dependent variable are within the categories of the independent variable (Nie et al. 1975:230). Eta is an asymmetric test which is designed for use when the independent variable is at the nominal level and the dependent variable is at the interval or ratio level (Nie et al. 1975:230). When the means of the categories of the independent variables are equal (Eta = 0), and if there is a large difference between the means, the Eta score advances to a maximum of 1 (Nie et al. 1975:230). The Eta test score when type is the independent variable and weight is the dependent variable is 0.7827. The score indicates a high degree of dissimilarity between the mean weights of the independent variable categories of type. Simply stated, there is a large difference in tool size as determined by weight between the different types of lithic tools at CdHk-3.

The second hypothesis tested was the correlation of lithic material and tool type. Because of the large sample, it was decided to use Cramer's $V$ for the initial comparison between type and material. Cramer's $V$ is a version of Phi modified for larger samples (Nie et al. 1975:224). Cramer's $V$ scores range from 0 to 1, where 0 equals no association and 1 equals a perfect association. A large $V$ score reveals a high degree of association without indicating how the variables are associated (Nie et al. 1975:225). A Cramer's $V$ of 0.53353 was obtained in the comparison of type by material. This score indicates a moderate degree of association between type and weight. On the basis of the Cramer's alone, a precise relationship between lithic raw material and the tool class could not be demonstrated. As a result, the asymmetric uncertainty coefficient was selected as a second test. The asymmetric uncertainty coefficient is "... the proportion by which 'uncertainty' in the dependent variable is reduced by a knowledge of the independent variable" (Nie et al. 1975:226). The uncertainty coefficient also works on a scale of 0 to 1, where 0 equals no improvement in ambiguity of the data and 1 equals a complete elimination of uncertainty (Nie et al. 1975:226). With type as the independent variable and material as the dependent variable, the uncertainty coefficient is 0.48016. A knowledge of type thus explains some of the ambiguity about the distribution of material, but there has not been more than a moderate reduction in the uncertainty about the distribution of material with regard to type. Given the moderate results from the Cramer's $V$ and the uncertainty coefficient, it is reasonable to conclude that tool type is affected by lithic raw material.

The third hypothesis proposes that tool use, determined by residue, is reflected by tool type. Because both residue and type are nominal variables, the Cramer's $V$ was used. A comparison of type and residue yielded a $V$ of 0.61326 indicating a moderate to strong association between type and residue or use. An asymmetric uncertainty coefficient test measuring "the proportional reduction in uncertainty which is gained by knowing the joint distribution of cases" (Nie et al. 1975:227) was chosen because neither type nor residue seemed an appropriate dependent variable. Rather, both variables were considered independent. This statistic indicated a relationship of 0.51801, which is interpreted as meaning that if the distribution of residues and types are known with regard to each other then the uncertainty of both in relation to each other is reduced. When the association between type and residues via the Cramer's $V$ and the Asymmetric Uncertainty Coefficient tests are considered together, a strong enough relationship exists to reject the null hypothesis, indicating that tool type is a function of tool use.

The fourth hypothesis assumes that tool type is influenced by the area of the site in which the tool was discarded. This hypothesis is based upon the assumption that tool type is both a functional and cultural variable. As one moves between activity areas and cultural horizons this variability should be manifest. Because both variables are nominal, the Cramer's $V$ was used to measure the strength of association. A $V$ of 0.65957 was recorded indicating a moderate to strong association between type and site area. In an Asymmetric Uncertainty Coefficient test with type as an independent variable and area as the dependent variable a correlation of 0.5866 was obtained. The establishment of a moderate to strong association between type and area in the $V$ test, and a moderate degree of uncertainty reduction in predicting type if area is known, allows a strong inference to be made that type varies with area across the site.

The fifth hypothesis assumes that the type of lithic material used in a tool influences the size of the tool. Material is a nominal variable and weight is an interval ratio variable. Given these variable types, a one-way Anova was run. The between-group $F$ test yielded an $F$ ratio of 8.101 (df = 6) which is significant at the 0.01 level. This highly significant $F$ score allows us to relate lithic material and tool size. A second test of association, an asymmetric Eta, was run to examine the mean weight (dependent variable) between the independent variable types of lithic raw materials present in tools on the site. The Eta score of 0.7580 indicates a high degree of variability between the mean weights of tools made from the eight different raw materials discussed earlier. The combination of the between-group $F$ and the Eta scores suggests that lithic material can be used to predict tool size.

The sixth hypothesis states that residue, as a reflection of tool use, is influenced by artifact size or weight. Residue is a nominal variable and weight an interval ratio one. With these variable types it is possible to use a one-way Anova. The between-group $F$ test of 1.238 (df = 9), is not significant at the 0.01 level. As a result, the null hypothesis is not rejected. This indicates that tool size does not influence use as evidenced by residue in the Foxie Otter sample.

The seventh hypothesis tested the variation of tool size by site area. The existence of substantial variability in gross artifact size across the site is one factor in postulating horizontal component separation. Site area is the nominal variable and weight is the interval ratio variable. Given these variables, a one-way Anova was used. The between-group $F$ test for weight and area yielded an $F$ ratio of 4.261 (df = 3) which is significant at 0.01. In an Eta test, however, a score of 0.4968 indicated that only a moderate degree of uncertainty is reduced for the independent variable by a knowledge of the dependent variable weight. Though we can reject the null hypothesis that area is not a factor in predicting tool size, the Eta score does not substantially reduce the uncertainty of the distribution of weight if area is known. This set of results, may reflect the fact that other variables (e.g., type and material) are factors in this relationship. It will be necessary to examine this possibility further when the tool analysis is synthesized.

The eighth hypothesis tested tool use by lithic raw material, based upon the assumption that the large graywacke core and quartzite flake tools are wood-working implements while the smaller chert and quartz implements are for skin and food preparation. Both residue and material are nominal variables. As with preceding pairs of nominal variables, the Cramer's $V$ and the asymmetric Eta were used to examine the strength of association and the reduction of uncertainty of material if residue is known. The $V$ score of 0.46095, indicates a weak to moderate association. An Eta score with residue as the independent and material as the dependent variable was only 0.300. The Eta indicates a very slight reduction of uncertainty in the distribution of material if residue type is known. With these results, it is not possible to infer that use is influenced by raw material.

The ninth hypothesis tested the variation of lithic raw material from site area to site area. An intuitive observation was made that chert, quartz and quartzite were prevalent in the Woodland occupations, and graywacke and small amounts of quartz were more common in the Archaic component. This resulted in a research hypothesis which states that there is significant variability in the lithic raw material types present on the site from one area to the next. Both variables are nominal. They were examined via the Cramer's $V$

and the asymmetric Eta tests. The *V* test showed a strong association of 0.70025 between material and area. This association is sufficient to reject the null hypothesis. However, when the Eta (0.2302) is examined, it is found that in a comparison with material as the independent and area as the dependent variable, only a small amount of uncertainty is removed about the distribution of the associated variables. This dichotomy between the results of the two tests is indicative of the fact that the association between material and site area is a more complex relationship than can be explained by the statistics used.

The last hypothesis tested a relationship between tool use and site area. The research hypothesis maintains that tool use varied between cultural horizons and activity areas. Rejection of the null hypothesis assumes that there is a significant difference in the residues found on the tools from one site area to the next. Both residue and area are nominal variables. Hence they are compared using the Cramer's *V* and the asymmetric Eta. The Cramer's *V* showed a weak to moderate association of 0.46714. Similarly, the Eta score of 0.200 indicates that very little uncertainty is removed when the independent variable residue and the dependent variable area are compared. This would indicate that the null hypothesis should not be rejected and that there were similar processing activities going on across the site.

On the basis of the tests described on the preceding pages, it can be suggested that there are significant relationships between tool form and tool use across the site. Accepting this premise, the stage is set for examining the tool assemblage from CdHk-3. Two broad categories, physical attributes and tool use, will be used. Of these, physical attributes show the most variability. Attributes will be considered both across the site and within localized areas. Significant variability was found across the site, between tool type, weight, and material. When site area was controlled, however, it was found that tool type, weight, and material showed significant associations within discrete site areas. These factors can be used to conclude that there is notable assemblage variability between site areas. The data further suggest that it is most pronounced between area D and areas A, B, C and E. This is in line with the assumption that area D represents an Archaic occupation, while Woodland period material predominates in the other four sectors.

Tool use is the second major category considered. Unlike tool attributes, a significant association is shown only between residue and type. This is interpreted as indicating that tool type at CdHk-3 reflects function. Bifaces generally have a wider range of blood, fat, starch and pitch, while multifaces and unifaces have combinations of pitch and fat. As a result, it is reasonable to state that bifaces are a more general tool, while multifaces and unifaces have more restricted functions that entail scraping hides and wood. In other comparisons between residue and weight, residue and material, and residue and area there is no association shown. This can be interpreted as meaning that tool size and the specific raw material from which a tool is made do not affect its function. Similarly, function does not vary significantly between site areas. By extrapolation, tool function does not vary significantly between occupations. The residue use analysis has demonstrated that tool type is the most important attribute when considering tool use at CdHk-3.

## Debitage Analysis

Debitage was encoded in attribute sets that could be used to predict primary forms of reduction. The two major types of debitage distinguished are *platform remnant bearing flakes* (PRB's) and *shatter*, or debris without any remnant of a striking platform (Magne n.d.:6). PRB's were further separated into lipped and nonlipped platform flakes. Lipped flakes are largely the product of bifacial reduction (Magne n.d.:13). They are produced when the platform-core face angle approaches 45 degrees (Magne 1978:68). Recent experimentation by the author has shown that lipped flakes can be produced with either a hard or soft hammer. The determining factors are the brittleness of the raw material and the relative hardness of the hammer to the material being worked. PRB flakes with platform angles of greater than 45 degrees are produced in the course of percussion flaking and are indicative of bifacial technology. Shatter was defined as either block or flake. Experimentally, a high percentage of block and flake shatter to platform flakes has been observed in the primary stages of bipolar reduction in experiments (Magne 1983:105–6). This observation is consistent with findings made by Binford, that cubic unsystematic angular fragments are common in the primary stages of bipolar reduction (1972:354). By observing significant frequencies of lipped flakes or large proportions of block and flake shatter in association with fractured pebble cores or bipolar flakes, inferences may be drawn concerning primary reduction strategies at the site (McPherron 1967:129). In controlling for bifacial and bipolar reduction, the primary lithic techniques utilized in the upper Great Lakes have been considered. Unfortunately, this level of discrimination can only be practiced at the level of primary reduction. Magne has observed that at latter stages of tool production, blanks produced by bipolar reduction are often further reduced by means of bifacial reduction (1983:106–7). Because of this, the analysis of reduction techniques is useful only at the primary level.

Based upon Pokotylo's (1978:208) experimental results and Magne's (1983:113) pilot study, weight was chosen as the most useful metric variable for debitage size.

During the 1980 and 1981 seasons 4,377 flakes were excavated at CdHk-3. Of that population 2,097, or 48%, were statistically analyzed. The total sample size was determined by the *N* of the Maxi Stat program which was used to analyze the collection (Walonick 1982).

Because of the differential density of debitage across the site, a stratified sampling strategy had to be used. Of the 4,377 flakes recovered, 596 (14% of the total sample) were from areas A, B, C, and E. Area D had 3,781, or 86%, of the total population. Because of the sparse distribution of flakes in areas A, B, C, and E, it was decided to use the entire sample of 596 flakes (28% of the analyzed sample). The remaining 1,501 flakes were randomly selected by quadrant and level from area D (72% of the analyzed sample). Given the scattered distribution of debitage between a number of activity areas, it was necessary to obtain adequate sample sizes from as many features as possible to insure that intrasite variability was adequately controlled.

For the debitage analysis, the interval ratio variable weight was turned into a nominal variable: 0–2 grams, 2.1–5 grams, and 5.1–150 grams (Table 11).

Six specific hypotheses were tested using the eight-segment typology described in Figure 16 and the metric weight measurement. The testing of these hypotheses is reported in Table 13.

The result of testing these six hypotheses has been the failure to reject the null hypothesis in three instances. The three hypotheses in which the null was not rejected are all concerned with the distribution of debitage by weight. It was thought when the hypotheses were formulated that areas of primary reduction would exhibit a larger range of flake sizes. This has not been born out by the research. Further, recent experiments with debitage variables by Magne (1983:125) have shown weight not to be a significant variable in reduction sequences. Weight was an attractive choice for a metric debitage variable because it gave a relative size to the often amorphous flakes without having to manipulate the multi-dimensions of length, width, and thickness. Unfortunately, this research simply confirms Magne's recent conclusions about weight. This removes a significant variable from the examination of reduction sequence.

The three variables in which the null were rejected provide us with some interesting possibilities in terms of intrasite variability for raw material usage and reduction type. The strongest of these is the high degree of variability between area D, in which graywacke was reduced, and the rest of the site where quartz, chert and quartzite predominated. Less significant was the comparison between all the site areas, which showed a moderate degree of variability between the five zones. Even in the Woodland areas of the site represented by areas A, B, C, and E there was not a uniform distribution of quartz, chert, and quartzite. For instance, the few pieces of quartzite found all came from area E on Otter Slide Island. Further, from hearth to hearth within the Woodland areas the same frequencies of chert, burnt chert and quartz did not appear. Unfortunately, the samples are often too small for

## TABLE 10
### Frequency of Lithic Raw Materials Found in Debitage

| Material | Number | Percent | %Burnt |
|---|---|---|---|
| 1 = vein quartz | 443 | 21.1 % | |
| 2 = quartzite | 7 | 0.3 % | |
| 3 = chert | 60 | 2.9 % | |
| 4 = graywacke | 1469 | 70.1 % | |
| 5 = burnt quartz | 4 | 0.2 % | 0.2 % |
| 6 = burnt quartzite | 5 | 0.2 % | 0.2 % |
| 7 = burnt chert | 107 | 5.1 % | 5.1 % |
| 8 = burnt graywacke | 2 | 0.1 % | 0.1 % |
| TOTAL | 2097 | 100.0 % | 5.6 % |

## TABLE 11
### Flake Type Frequencies

| Artifact Type | Number | Percent | Platform vs. Shatter | |
|---|---|---|---|---|
| 1 = lip flake cortex | 21 | 1.0% | 18.5% | |
| 2 = lip flake without | 368 | 17.5% | | 24.1% |
| 3 = PRB cortex | 21 | 1.0% | 5.6% | |
| 4 = PRB without | 96 | 4.6% | | |
| 5 = block shatter cortex | 23 | 1.1% | 11.3% | |
| 6 = block shatter without | 214 | 10.2% | | 75.8% |
| 7 = flake cortex | 78 | 3.7% | 64.5% | |
| 8 = flake without | 1276 | 60.8% | | |
| TOTAL | 2097 | 100.0% | 100.0% | 100.0% |

## TABLE 12
### Breakdown of Debitage Weight

Minimum = 0 (i.e. less than .1 gram)
Maximum = 124
Range = 124
Sum = 2136
Mean = 1.019
Median = .2
Mode = 0
Variance = 13.97
Standard Deviation = 3.738
Standard error of the mean = .082
95% Confidence Interval = .859 - 1.179
99% Confidence Interval = .808 - 1.229

## Analysis of CdHk-3

TABLE 13
Hypotheses for Debitage Tested via the Cramer's V*

1. AREA vs. WEIGHT
   *Null:* Debitage size does not vary significantly between site areas.
   *Research:* There is a significant variability in debitage weight between site areas.

   The null hypothesis was not rejected.

2. AREA vs. MATERIAL
   *Null:* Raw material does not vary by site area.
   *Research:* Raw material does vary by site area.

   There were two Cramer's V tests performed. The first was on site areas A-E where the Cramer's V score was .504. The second test was performed on data with Areas A, B, C, and E collapsed against Area D. The score was .915.

   The null hypothesis was rejected.

3. AREA vs. FLAKE TYPE
   *Null:* Flake type does not vary by site area.
   *Research:* Flake type does vary by site area.

   The null hypothesis was rejected despite a weak association.

4. WEIGHT vs. MATERIAL
   *Null:* Debitage weight does not vary due to lithic raw material.
   *Research:* Debitage weight does vary due to lithic raw material.

   The null hypothesis was not rejected.

5. WEIGHT vs. FLAKE TYPE
   *Null:* Weight does not vary due to flake type.
   *Research:* Weight does vary due to flake type.

   The null hypothesis was not rejected.

6. RAW MATERIAL vs. FLAKE TYPE
   *Null:* Flake type does not vary due to raw material type.
   *Research:* Flake type does vary due to raw material type.

   The null hypothesis was rejected but the pattern was very weak.

*Actual Cramer's V scores appear in Table 14.

TABLE 14
Cramer's V Scores

|            | AREA | WEIGHT | MATERIAL         | FLAKE TYPE |
|------------|------|--------|------------------|------------|
| Area       | -    | 0.098  | 0.504 + <br> 0.915* | 0.392   |
| Weight     | -    | -      | 0.080            | 0.160      |
| Material   | -    | -      | -                | 0.275      |
| Flake type | -    | -      | -                | -          |

+ without graywacke
* total sample

anything more than a subjective observation, but at this level there is some degree of variability in the presence of locally available quartz and the imported "Michigan" cherts. The majority of this chert appears to have been heat-treated, which may be indicative of improving the working characteristics of a scarce commodity to maximize its usage (Rich 1978:1). This contrasts with graywacke, quartz and quartzite which are all locally available and show little evidence of heat treatment (See Table 10 for a breakdown).

Another factor is the very low frequency of locally available graywacke outside the Early Archaic component in area D. It is further suggested that one of the defining factors of the Archaic assemblage at the site is the restricted distribution of the graywacke to area D. Graywacke is as locally abundant as quartz. It is possible to speculate that it does not appear in the other areas due to cultural preference, not geographic distribution. This contrasts with chert which is imported and locally scarce. In its absence, the local materials, quartz and quartzite may have been utilized instead.

The other two hypotheses where the null was rejected or partially rejected illustrate very weak associations, but when they are considered together they represent an interesting trend. Hypothesis three examined site area and flake type. The rejection of the null hypothesis (Table 11) indicates flake type variation between site areas. The predominant flaking technique on the site is bifacial reduction which is represented by three successive stages of tool manufacture and regeneration: primary, secondary, and tertiary flaking of both cores and flakes. The prevalence of bifacial or lipped flakes, the remains of cortex on some flakes, and a low number of overlapping flake scars on the graywacke bifaces indicate that area D represents the primary and secondary bifacial reduction of graywacke. In areas A, B, C and E most of the evidence indicates tertiary bifacial reduction. The presence of block and flake shatter does, however, indicate that some bipolar reduction of chert and quartz took place.

The sixth hypothesis maintains that flake type does not vary with lithic raw material. On the basis of a weak pattern (Cramer's $V = 0.275$) the null could not be summarily rejected. The failure to totally reject the null that flake type does not vary with raw material is the result of block and flake shatter being more evident among chert and quartz than graywacke or quartzite on this site. Subjectively, this supports the observation that bipolar reduction is evident in the Woodland and not the Archaic components. The trends in both hypotheses five and six are so weak that their interpretation is extremely subjective.

In summary, the flake analysis indicates that the principal form of reduction on the site was bifacial. Both the tools and debitage from the Archaic concentration in area D indicate primary and secondary bifacial reduction. In Woodland areas A, B, C and E, bifacial rethinning and sharpening appear to have been predominant. There is some evidence for bipolar reduction in the Woodland components. The end result of the debitage analysis was weakened by the negation of the metric variable weight. With the size variable inoperative, the subsequent interpretations are not very strong, but still useful.

# 5
# Summary and Conclusions

## The Sequence of Occupation

Lenard Mousseau, a lifelong trapper on the Spanish River, speaks of the rotting remains of birchbark sap buckets he found in a maple grove across Fox Lake from the Foxie Otter site in the years immediately before the First World War (1980: personal communication). Those buckets are the last physical remains of native occupations at Fox Lake which reach back approximately 7,670 years.

On the site itself, a single glass seed bead found in loose context with a moose calcaneus (see Appendix 1) testifies to occupation in the post-European contact period.

Prehistoric remains excavated from the site indicate two major periods of occupation—Woodland and Early Archaic. The range of C-14 dates from CdHk-3 indicate a Terminal Woodland occupation during the period A.D. 1260 to 1580 (Wright 1972:64). This occupation is corroborated by the discovery of a small triangular quartz projectile point that Wright describes as late Terminal Woodland (1980: personal communication) and by a small body sherd of grit-tempered pottery situated next to a hearth dated at A.D. 1260. The other small side-notched projectile points have been identified by J. V. Wright and T. Conway (1982 and 1981: personal communication) as the transitional period between Initial and Terminal Woodland prior to A.D. 1000.

It is impossible to know for certain, but it can be inferred that the Terminal Woodland occupants were the ancestors of the Archirigouans (Bass people) reported by the Jesuit missionaries to have lived near the mouth of the Spanish River in the seventeenth century (Thwaites 1901:(33)149; Hanks 1981:183). According to the Jesuits, the Archirigouans were involved in a trade between the Huron and the Cree (Thwaites 1901:(44)243). Oral histories from Ojibwa and Ottawa at Sagamok, collected by the author, suggest that the Spanish River was a canoe route from Lake Huron over the height-of-land to the James Bay drainage in historic times (Hanks 1981:26). This is corroborated by John McBean's 1827 map of the north shore of Lake Huron (PAC, HBCA, D.5/2, fo. 257), and the distribution of sites in the Spanish system (Hanks 1981:181–85) The presence of imported cherts which resemble material from the "Michigan Peninsula" in the Woodland component argues strongly that the late prehistoric people, like their historic descendants, were involved in long distance travel or trade on the upper Great Lakes. A high level of group mobility is also suggested by the predominance of small resharpening flakes and a lack of discarded tools, in the Woodland components, indicative of a highly curated technology (Stevenson 1984: personal communication).

The second major cultural sequence present at the Foxie Otter site is the Early Archaic component. The Archaic assemblage is predominated by locally available graywacke utilized in large bifaces and scrapers. By marked contrast to the Woodland components, large graywacke bifacial thinning flakes and discarded core tools indicate a technology that has a local source of raw material and requires little or no curation. With the exception of a few flakes of graywacke found along the bank edge in front of the Moose Run cabin, the evidence for the reduction and utilization of graywacke is restricted to the north end of the 38° baseline. One dense concentration of primary and secondary debitage was located in conjunction with a possible hearth. A scattered veneer of debitage exists over a broad area suggesting artifact displacement and possibly the existence of other foci of lithic reduction.

The predominance of locally available, low quality lithic material in the Archaic component suggests less intraregional mobility of groups than was evident in the Woodland components.

The second major activity area slightly south of the graywacke concentration is a diffuse scatter of red ochre fragments mixed with flakes. In the center of this area, a small pit was located. This feature was dated at $7670 \pm 120$ B.P. When this date is considered with the flotation data, which suggest that the site is not older than approximately 7,000 years, it is reasonable to assume the site was first occupied at the time of the white pine maximum.

The Foxie Otter site has been occupied at least three times over the last 7,000 years. The present evidence indicates that the intensity and/or frequency of this usage increased during Terminal Woodland times after roughly A.D. 1250 and continued into the historic period. This discovery fills a gap in the archaeological record which was perceived during earlier surveys of the Spanish River. At that time, all the sites located were aceramic (Hanks 1981:179–80). The presence of a large multicomponent site at the Fox Lake end of the portage to the Spanish River, and the smaller CdHk-1 at the other end on the elbow of the river, corresponds to a phenomenon found elsewhere on the Spanish River: that lakes were used for subsistence and living, while the river was used as a transportation corridor (Hanks 1981:181–82). The Early Archaic trihedral adze found at the elbow indicates usage of that site during the white pine maximum (Fox 1980:123). Established at an early date, the lake-river distribution pattern evident on the Spanish and many other river and lake systems of the Canadian Shield continues through the historic period.

## Subsistence

Residue analysis indicates that the processing of animal products (i.e., cutting raw and cooked meat, and scraping hides) was the most frequent activity. There is a very low frequency of hunting equipment, specifically projectile points. This may indicate that kills were made elsewhere and brought back to the site. Wright has questioned this interpretation, noting that "if game was brought back along with damaged hunting gear there should be a bunch of projectile points lying about" (1987: personal communication). It could also suggest the curation of hunting equipment or that other procurement methods such as snares[6] were being used.

Traces of plant fibers are common on multipurpose tools. They are, however, largely associated with hafting and wood-working as opposed to plant processing. This trend is drawn out by the flotation data which suggest the utilization of hazelnut, pin cherry, raspberries and elderberries in small quantities during a summer-fall occupation. The low density of gathered seeds is further consistent with Cleland's (1982:265) observation that plant resources were far more restricted north of the Great Lakes than to the south where they were an important dietary item. It is also evidence of the poor organic preservation in the northern forest.

At a very low level of generalization, Foxie Otter may be described as a summer-fall camp where meat and hides were processed.

## Lithic Technology

There are a number of sources of variability between the Woodland and Archaic components with regard to lithic reduction and tool manufacture. In the Archaic reduction area, large pieces of tabular graywacke were being bifacially reduced. A combination of bipolar and bifacial reduction of smaller cobbles of quartz and the bifacial thinning of frequently fire-treated chert predominated in the Woodland zones.

In both the Archaic and Woodland components lithic reduction was normally done in general activity areas (e.g., near hearths and aggregations of fire-cracked rock, which may be indicative of house structures). At the present level of analysis, it is not possible to segregate stone tool preparation

---

[6]Babiche snares were until recently used by Cree and Athapaskan hunters for moose, caribou, and mountain sheep.

spatially from other generalized domestic activities. This corroborates that activity areas are nearly all multifunctional (Yellen 1977; Janes 1983).

As a general rule across the site, the usage patterns of bifaces differed significantly from the usage of multifaces or unifaces. The bifaces were associated with blood, fat, starch and pitch, while multifaces and unifaces more frequently contained evidence of pitch and fat. This is characteristic of cutting vs. scraping functions. The predominant tool form must be considered "expedient" as opposed to "stylized." This appears to reflect processing as opposed to hunting activities. The observation that type denotes function appears to hold across the Woodland classification.

Archaic tools differ significantly from Woodland tools in size. Archaic graywacke tools are larger and lack evidence of significant tertiary refitting. The Woodland tools are much smaller and show considerable evidence of repeated retouch. This may be partially explained by the conservation of a scarce resource, nonlocal chert. On the basis of these observations, it is proposed that tool size is, at least partially, a culturally determined factor in that decisions were made about the curation or discarding of usable items. Expedient tool types are a function of use.

## Regional Perspective

Placing the Foxie Otter site within a regional perspective is complicated by the predominance of expedient tools. The lack of stylized diagnostics makes the normal process of typological comparison on an intersite basis difficult for the Woodland and impossible for the Early Archaic.

Traces of the Early Archaic in the upper Great Lakes are generally scarce, probably due to low human population levels during that time (Mason 1981:131; Fitting 1975:67). In addition, the flooding of the Lake Stanley beach ridges during the rise of Lake Nipissing may have wiped out some sites that did exist (Mason 1981:131–32; Fitting 1975:67). Prior to recent work on the Spanish River system, only two Early Archaic components north of Lake Huron had been discovered. Both locations were in loose association with late Paleo-Indian remains at the George Lake and Sheguiandah quarries (Mason 1981:129; Greenman 1943; Lee 1957). A third Early Archaic possibility is Storck's Lamorandiere Bay site near George Lake, given its location on a high beach ridge and the presence of relatively large bifacially flaked preforms (1974:10–13). Because of the associations with lithic quarrying as opposed to subsistence activities at two of the three locations it is difficult to understand them in terms of seasonal round. Further, only rough dates have been accepted for the Archaic usage of the quarries. The sparse evidence of Archaic people in the area north of Lake Huron during the period of very rapid environmental and geographic change in the postglacial period has led to the decision to follow Mason's lead and collapse the distinction between the Early and Middle Archaic when dealing with the upper Great Lakes (1981:126-27). Until further research justifies a more refined approach, the Archaic occupations between roughly 8000 and 5500 B.P. will be lumped into the Early Archaic. This period begins at the end of the late Paleo-Indian times and passes with the dramatic flowering of the Late Archaic in more or less modern environmental conditions.

Notched, stemmed and shouldered projectile points have normally been used as the diagnostic indicators of the Early Archaic (Mason 1981:129; Wright 1978:73; Fitting 1975:65). On the Spanish system, there are three sites that have been linked with the Early Archaic. At CdHk-1 a trihedral adze was found. These are normally associated with the white pine maximum (Fox 1980). CdHk-3 (7690 ± 120 B.P.) and CcHl-2 (5910 ± 115 B.P.) have charcoal dates in context with flakes (Hanks 1981:152). More significantly, none of these sites were quarries or located on fossil beach ridges. Of the three sites, one was on an interior lake and two at portages on the Spanish River. All three locations were at spots that could have been or were multiply utilized by later occupants.

This interior distribution makes sense given Fitting's (1975:64) interpretation of the Early Archaic peoples as hunters, gatherers and fishing people, and Cleland's (1982:768) suggestion that evidence from the northern Great Lakes indicated that Archaic people were primarily hunters for whom fishing filled minor role. If Early Archaic people were fishing intensively, a point for which Cleland (1982:768) acknowledges there is absolutely no evidence, then it would have been during spring spawning runs with spears, weirs, and/or by angling in shallow shoals and in rapids and river shallows (Cleland 1982). If this were the case, then it might be expected that many of the Early Archaic fishing sites would be found at fossil river mouths now submerged under Lake Huron. The other option would be locations on the streams and rivers above Nipissing shores on the Canadian Shield edge, where weirs might have been established. Unfortunately, portage sites at rapids and falls on the northern interior drainage of Lake Huron have often been re-used and lack sufficient soil development to distinguish different occupations. Frequently, forest fires make carbon dating difficult if not impossible. Finally, the erosional regime of many rivers makes for rather poor site preservation. Hence, it is not a simple matter to identify Early Archaic components in the interior.

The sites in the Spanish River drainage seem to cluster between the beginning of the white pine maximum and the establishment of the Late Archaic, circa 5500 B.P. (3500 B.C.). This roughly corresponds to the Ritchie-Fitting hypothesis which maintains that there was an acceleration in population growth with the advent of the white pine maximum (Mason 1981:182). Unfortunately, several small, dispersed sites do not establish a population expansion. They could as well be explained by the passage of several very small groups over a long period of time.

The Archaic tool assemblage at the Foxie Otter site consists of relatively large, expedient core tools. This suggests a pattern when compared with the quantities of bifacial tools or preforms at George Lake and Sheguiandah and the large bifacial thinning flakes from CcHl-2 (Hanks 1982:171). One must question whether the large bifaces that characterize the quarries are really only preforms. The evidence from the Spanish suggests they are large core tools that were thinned over time as refitting was required. This leads to the conclusion that, although large bificial tools are not restricted to the Early Archaic, they are certainly a significant indicator of it.

Despite the tentativeness of most interpretations, the proposed Early Archaic component at CdHk-3 leaves one to consider an inland pattern of dispersement for the Early Archaic, away from beach ridges where it has been traditionally sought. Further, it has been suggested that the large bifaces form a basic part of Early Archaic assemblages and are not simply preforms. These patterns will require more refinement and testing before they can be uncritically accepted. It is hoped, however, they will stimulate a reconsideration of the Early Archaic north of Lake Huron.

The other major component of CdHk-3 belongs to the Terminal Woodland. The evidence indicates that the site was a summer-fall hunting camp. This corresponds well with Cleland's (1982) reconstruction of Late Woodland subsistence in the northern Great Lakes. The seasonal timing of these occupations indicates that the Woodland people could have been at the inshore fisheries at Fox Lake between the spring and late fall. Cleland (1982) has demonstrated that this was fundamental to Woodland subsistence strategy. Further, the evidence from the Foxie Otter site potentially contributes to the proposal of a seasonal round for the Terminal Woodland period whereby bands moved down to Lake Huron during the spring and fall to fish and withdrew into the interior to hunt and gill-net fish on small interior lakes at other times. This cycle would fit with Cleland's hypothesized pattern of population aggregation and dispersion for the Middle and Late Woodland (1982:780).

## Conclusion

Only a small part of CdHk-3 has been excavated, but the evidence to date offers a number of new directions for research in the Spanish system and in the area north of Lake Huron in general. At times the data have been pushed to their logical limits in order to stress the potential of small, dispersed site

## Summary and Conclusions 75

archaeology. Deeply stratified sites are rare in the northern forest. Consequently, if we are to understand the aboriginal occupation north of the Great Lakes on the Shield edge, it is necessary to look at small sites in terms of the drainage and the region in which they are found. Continuing progress on the north shore depends upon a research approach which recognizes this fact.

The problems confronted at the Foxie Otter site are typical of the northern forest. Methodologies utilized in this analysis to separate components using type, material, residue and area can provide a model for identifying divergent technologies across the horizontal distribution of a site. When these concepts are combined with recently improved methods of debitage analysis, it will be possible to begin consistently separating previously problematic mixed assemblages.

# References Cited

Acres Consulting Services
   1978   Spanish River Site 4 Feasibility Report. Niagara Falls: Acres Consulting Services Ltd.

Arundale, W. H.
   1980   Functional analysis of three unusual assemblages from the Cape Dorset area, Baffin Island. Arctic 33(3):404–86.

Bertulli, M. M.
   1981   Mississagi River with Many Mouths. Archaeological Survey of Laurentian University 9. Sudbury: Laurentian University.

Bigsby, John
   1850   The Shoe and Canoe or Pictures of Travel in Canada. New York: Paladin Press.

Binford, Lewis R.
   1972   An Archaeological Perspective. New York: Seminar Press.

Binford, Lewis R., and George Quimby
   1972   Indian sites and chipped stone materials in the northern Lake Michigan area. In: An Archaeological Perspective, L. Binford (ed.), pp. 346–72. New York: Seminar Press.

Boissonneau, A.
   1968   Glacial history of northeastern Ontario II: The Timiskaming-Algoma area. Canadian Journal of Earth Sciences 5(97):97–109.

Buchner, Anthony
   1981   Sinnock: A Paleolithic Camp and Kill Site in Manitoba. Papers in Manitoba Archaeology 10. Winnipeg: Department of Cultural Affairs and Historic Resources.

Callender, Charles
   1978   Great Lakes-Riverine sociopolitical organization. In: Handbook of North American Indians 15, B. G. Trigger (ed.), pp. 610–21. Washington: Smithsonian Institution.

Cleland, Charles
   1982   The inland shore fishery of the northern Great Lakes: Its development and importance in prehistory. American Antiquity 47(4):761–84.

   1966   The Prehistoric Animal Ecology and Ethnozoology of the Upper Great Lakes Region. Anthropological Papers, 29. The University of Michigan Museum of Anthropology. Ann Arbor.

Conway, T.
   1980   Heartland of the Ojibway. In: Collected Archaeological Papers, Archaeological Research Report 13., D. S. Melvin (ed.), pp. 29–64. Historical Planning and Research Branch, Toronto. Ontario Ministry of Culture and Recreation.

Fitting, James
   1975   The Archaeology of Michigan. Bloomfield Hills, Michigan: Cranbrook Institute of Science.

Fox, W.
  1980  The trihedral adze in Northwestern Ontario. In: Collected Archaeological Papers, Archaeological Research Report 13, D. Melvin (ed.), pp. 117–26. Historical Planning and Research Branch, Ontario Ministry of Culture and Recreation. Toronto.

Greenman, Emerson, and G. Stanley
  1943  The archaeology and geology of two early sites near Killarney, Ontario. Papers of the Michigan Academy off Science, Arts and Letters, 28: 505–31.

Hanks, Christopher
  1981  The Archaeology of the Spanish River. Jointly published by INCo Metals and the Ministry of Culture and Recreation. Sudbury.

Hannila, J.
  1979  Geology of the Spanish River Project. Sudbury: INCo Metals.

Hobson, Katherine, and D. Nelson
  1983  Simon Fraser University radiocarbon dates II. Radiocarbon 25(3):899–907.

Hough, John N.
  1966  Correlation of glacial lake stages in the Huron-Erie and Michigan basins. Journal of Geology, 74: 62–79.

Huntley, D.
  1981  An Introduction to Dating, Analysis and Location in Archaeology. Burnaby: Simon Fraser University.

Janes, Robert R.
  1983  Archaeological Ethnography Among MacKenzie Basin Dene, Canada. The Arctic Institute of North America. Technical Paper 28. Calagary: Arctic Institute.

Kalowicz, F., and R. Pammett
  1968  Archaeological site survey report: La Cloche. On file at the Historical Planning and Research Branch, Ministry of Culture and Recreation. Toronto.

Kam-Biu Liu and Audrey Davis
  1981  Postglacial environmental changes in northern Ontario as reflected by pollen and varve-sedimentary records from a meromictic Lake. Paper presented at the Association of American Geographers, Los Angeles.

Keeley, Lawrence
  1980  Experimental Determination of Stone Tool Uses. Chicago: The University of Chicago Press.

Kelly, Raymond, and William R. Farrand
  1967  The glacial lakes around Michigan. Geological Survey Bulletin, 4. Department of Conservation, State of Michigan. Lansing, Michigan.

Lee, Thomas
  1957  The antiquity of the Sheguiandah site. The Canadian Field Naturalist 71(3):117–35.

Lewis, Charlton T.
  1970  Recent uplift of Manitoulin Island, Ontario. Canadian Journal of Earth Science 7:665–75.

Magne, M.
 1983 Lithics and Livelihood: Stone Tool Technologies of Central and Interior British Columbia. Unpublished Ph. D. dissertation. The University of British Columbia, Vancouver.

 1978 Variability among four Archaic lithic assemblages in the Porcupine Mountain region, Manitoba. Unpublished M.A. thesis. The University of Manitoba, Winnipeg.

Mason, Ronald J.
 1981 Great Lakes Archaeology. New York: Academic Press.

McPherron, A.
 1967 The Juntunen Site and the Late Woodland Prehistory of the Upper Great Lakes Area. Anthropology Papers, 10. The University of Michigan Museum of Anthropology. Ann Arbor.

Mitchell, E. A.
 1977 Fort Timiskaming and the Fur Trade. Toronto: University of Toronto Press.

Nie, Norman, C. Hull, J. Jenkins, K. Steinbrenner and D. Bent
 1975 Statistical Package for the Social Sciences. New York: McGraw-Hill.

Ogden, I., and J. Gordon.
 1977 The Late Quaternary paleoenvironmental record of northeastern North America. In: Amerinds and Their Paleo-Environments in Northeastern North America, W. Newman and B. Salwen (eds.). Annals of the New York Academy of Science, 288:16–34.

Pokotylo, D.
 1978 Lithic Technology and Settlement Patterns in Upper Hat Creek Valley, B.C. Unpublished Ph. D. dissertation. The University of British Columbia, Vancouver.

Rich, J. W.
 1978 Heat Altered Cherts of the Lower Illinois Valley: An Experimental Study in Prehistoric Technology. Northwestern University Archaeological Program Prehistoric Records, 2. Evanston: Northwestern University.

Ritchie, William A.
 1980 The Archaeology of New York State. Harrison: Harbor Hill Books.

Rogers, Edward S.
 1978 Southeastern Ojibwa. In: Handbook of North American Indians 15, B. G. Trigger (ed.), pp. 760–71. Washington: Smithsonian Institution.

Saarnisto, M.
 1975 Stratigraphical studies on the shoreline displacement of Lake Superior. Canadian Journal of Earth Science, 12:100–39.

Storck, Peter L.
 1974 Two probable Shield Archaic sites in Killarney Provinicial Park, Ontario. Ontario Archaeology, 21:3–21.

Thomas, David H.
 1976 Figuring Anthropology: First Principles of Probability and Statistics. New York: Holt, Rinehart and Winston.

Thwaites, Reuben G.
 1901 The Jesuit Relations and Allied Documents: Travels and Explorations of the Jesuit Missionaries in New France 1610–1791. Cleveland: The Burrows Brothers Company.

Tringham, Ruth, G. Cooper, G. Odell, B. Voytek, and A. Whitman.
  1974  Experimentation in the formation of edge damage: A new approach to lithic analysis. Journal of Field Archaeology, 1:171–96.

Walonick, O.
  1981  Maxi-Stat. Longwood: Scott Adams Inc.

Waterbalk, H. T.
  1971  Working with radiocarbon dates. Proceedings of the Prehistoric Society, 37:15–33.

Wright, J. V.
  1978  The implications of probable Early and Middle Archaic projectile points from southern Ontario. Canadian Journal of Archaeology, 2:59–78.

  1972  Ontario Prehistory: An Eleven Thousand Year Archaeological Outline. Ottawa: National Museum of Man.

Yellen, John E.
  1977  Archaeological Approaches to the Present: Models for Reconstructing the Past. New York: Academic Press.

## MANUSCRIPTS

PAM, HBCA-D.5/2, fo. 257. John McBean Map, 1827.
PAC, HBCA-D.25/4, fo. 70.

# Appendix 1
# FAUNAL ANALYSIS OF THE FOXIE OTTER SITE

*by*
*Norman Haywood*

Of the 427 bone fragments recovered from the Foxie Otter site, 98.6% are calcined. Calcined bone is typically very fragmentary. It ranges in color from white to brown to blue. Since it is so fragmentary, identification of species is usually very difficult. The only positive species-level faunal identification from the Foxie Otter site was an unburned moose calcaneus (feature 1). The sustentaculum and the facet for the lateral malleolous had both been cut off. However, due to the deteriorating condition of the bone, it was impossible to detect any cut marks in these areas. From the calcined bone it was possible to tentatively identify porcupine or beaver, martin, and a canine from a Canid. All the faunal materials are from mammals. There are no bird or fish bones present.

Very few studies have been done on calcined bone. Lewis Binford did a comparative study on burned bones using dry human bones from a 1500 year old burial and green bone from a fresh monkey cadaver.[1] After burning the bones, he noticed "straight cracking...on the dry bone...[and] checking was superficial." The green bone both with and without flesh showed "deep transverse fractures, frequently curved, [and] much warping" after being burned. This latter fracturing is typical of the calcined bones recovered from the Foxie Otter site, indicating it was likely green bone, possibly with flesh attached, rather than dry bone. Binford concludes that "the degree of bone calcining is a function of the length of time in the fire, the intensity of the heat, the thickness of the protecting muscle tissue, and the position of the bone in relation to the point of oxidation of the consuming flame." Unfortunately, no studies have been done to determine how much time is required in different intensities of heat to calcined bones. John Driver (personal communication) has suggested that in order to have calcined bones, such as those from the Foxie Otter site, an intentional burning is required rather than an accidental burning such as that associated with a forest fire.

---

[1] *An Archaeological Perspective*, by Lewis R. Binford. 1972. New York: Seminar Press. Citations are from pages 375, 376.

TABLE 1.1
Catalog of Faunal Remains from the Foxie Otter Site

| Cat. # | Species | Element | Side | Comments |
|---|---|---|---|---|
| B-81-2 | v. large mammal | 2 frag. | - | - |
| B-81-3 | m. mammal | 13 frag. | - | calcined |
| B-81-4 | m. mammal | 18 frag. | - | calcined |
| B-81-5 | l. mammal | occipital condyle frag. | - | calcined |
| B-81-6 | m. mammal | 27 frag. | - | calcined |
| B-81-6 | poss. *Castor canadencis* or *Erthezon dorsatus* | occipital condyle | right | calcined |
| B-81-6 | m. mammal | inferior articulating processes of lumbar vert. | - | calcined |
| B-81-7 | m. mammal | skull fragment? | - | calcined |
| B-81-7 | m. mammal | 143 frag.? | - | calcined |
| B-81-8 | beaver or porcupine? | distal end of a metapodial | - | calcined |
| B-81-8 | m. mammal | 113 frag. | - | calcined |
| B-81-9 | mammal | 1 frag. | - | - |
| B-81-10 | m. mammal | 1 frag. | - | calcined |
| B-81-11 | m. mammal | 1 frag. | - | calcined |
| B-81-12 | m. mammal | 18 frag. | - | calcined |
| B-81-13 | martin ? | distal end of humerus | left | calcined |
| B-81-13 | s./m. mammal | metapodial | - | calcined |
| B-81-13 | m. mammal | 46 frag. | - | calcined |
| B-81-14 | m. mammal | 1 frag. | - | calcined |
| B-81-15 | m. mammal | 8 frag. | - | calcined |
| B-81-16 | m. mammal | 1 frag. | - | appears to be cut longitudinally |

## Appendix 1

| | | | | |
|---|---|---|---|---|
| B-81-17 | Canid (dog)? | canine | right | calcined |
| B-81-17 | m./l. mammal | 17 frag. | - | calcined |
| B-81-18 | m. mammal | 6 frag. | - | calcined |
| B-81-19 | mammal | 1 frag. | - | calcined |
| B-81-20 | mammal | 1 frag. | - | calcined |
| B-81-1 | *Alces alces* (moose) | calcaneus | left | sustentaculum and facet for lateral malleolus cut off |

# Appendix 2
## ARCHAEOBOTANICAL REMAINS FROM THE FOXIE OTTER SITE

*by*
*Rodolphe David Fecteau and John H. McAndrews*

*Royal Ontario Museum, Toronto*

## Macrofossil Analysis

Sixty-nine soil samples from the Foxie Otter site were submitted by Christopher Hanks for plant macrofossil identification in April of 1981. Two samples were not analyzed: sample 15, which contained two lithic fragments, and sample 69, in which the bag had disintegrated.

The following is the archaeological context of the soil samples. Samples 13, 16, 17, 37 and 68 were hearth samples; samples 2, 3, 9, 38, 43, 44, 51, 52, and 53 were feature samples; samples 1, 4–7, 10, 11, 12, 14, 18–36, 38–42, 45–50, 54–57, 66, and 67 were quadrant and level or depth samples; samples 58 through 65 were soil comparative samples.

## Method

Ten large soil samples (4, 17, 30, 31, 33, 34, 35, 36, 47,and 57) were floated using a SMAP machine (Watson 1976). Remaining soil samples (approximately one cubic liter each) were concentrated by dry sieving with a 9.5, 6.3 and 0.5 mm mesh.

Floated samples produced a light fraction that is included in this report. The dense material that sank was not analyzed.

Carbonized seeds were picked from float and soil residue under 10× magnification with a stereomicroscope. Uncarbonized seeds and other plant remains were identified but not picked, except for unknowns. Seeds were identified using seed identification manuals (Montgomery 1977: Martin and Barkley 1973) and by comparison with reference specimens.

Carbonized wood was prepared for examination by breaking the specimen to obtain a fresh transverse (cross) section and was identified using an illustrated wood charcoal identification key (McAndrews et al.) and by comparison with reference specimens. Identification was made under magnification of $7\times$ to $40\times$.

## Seeds

The concentrate was mostly mineral soil particles. The organic material was carbonized and uncarbonized plant debris, such as wood, leaf fragments and roots.

A total of 11,178 ml of float and dry soil residue was examined. This yielded 157 seeds; 146 (8 taxa) were uncarbonized and 11 (4 taxa) were carbonized (Table 2.1).

Carbonized seeds or seed fragments of pin cherry, raspberry, elderberry, hazelnut and unknowns were present in samples 8, 13, 14, 19, 23, 28, 40, 47, 51, 57 and 66. Uncarbonized seeds of birch, hazelnut, knotweed, pin cherry, raspberry, cedar, *Viola* and unknowns were present in 39 of 69 samples.

The carbonized seeds were confined to the cultural soil samples. Only uncarbonized seeds were present in the comparative (control) samples.

## Carbonized Wood

Some fragments were large enough to identify, but most were too small (less than 5 mm) for positive identification.

A total of 36.0 g of carbonized wood were examined from 38 samples (Table 2.2).

Carbonized wood from 38 samples was classified into seven categories: (1) maple, (2) birch, (3) poplar/willow, (4) indeterminable diffuse porous, (5) pine, (6) indeterminable conifer wood, and (7) indeterminable. Pine and indeterminable conifer were the most abundant. Poplar/willow, birch and maple were the less abundant hardwoods.

Pine wood makes up the largest portion of carbonized wood examined (52.5%). Small amounts of poplar/willow (13.8%), maple (1.1%) and birch (.6%) were also identified. Partially identified wood amounted to 26.1% and 5.8%. Small amounts of pine wood was identified in control samples 59 and 65. Pine wood was present in hearth samples 17 and 68 and maple wood was identified in hearth sample 68.

## Discussion

The fossil seeds and carbonized wood are all derived from plants that are native to the site: no fossils of introduced plants were identified. Raspberry, elderberry, and knotweed are weedy and thrive on sites disturbed by humans. Birch, hazelnut and pin cherry flourish after forest fires. Thus some of the fossils could be the result of twentieth century disturbance. However, because the control samples lacked the carbonized seeds that were present in the cultural samples, except hearths, we infer that at least some of the carbonized seeds are contemporaneous with prehistoric occupation.

The uncarbonized fossils suggest intrusion of modern seeds into prehistoric soil levels and features.

Hazelnut, pin cherry, raspberry and elderberry are edible. If the prehistoric inhabitants had gathered these fruits this would indicate a summer-fall occupation. The sparseness of edible fruit remains suggests casual rather than intensive use.

The fossil flora is consistent with the vegetation of the past 7,000 years and no further chronological refinement can be made.

The presence of carbonized wood in the control samples suggests that some of the fossil carbonized wood could be intrusive. The lack of carbonized wood in the three "hearth" samples casts doubt that these features actually were hearths.

ACKNOWLEDGMENTS

We thank Christine Caroppo for critical assessment and Linda White who typed the manuscript.

REFERENCES

McAndrews, J. H., R. D. Fecteau, and S. A. Hick
   n.d.   Archaeobotany in Ontario. Manuscript.

Martin, A. C., and W. D. Barkley
   1973   Seed Identification Manual. Berkeley: University of California Press.

Montgomery, F. H.
   1977   Seeds and Fruits of Plants of Eastern Canada and Northeastern United States. Toronto: University of Toronto Press.

Panshin, A. J., and C. de Zeeuw
   1970   Textbook of Wood Technology. Structure, Identification and Properties of Commercial Woods of United States and Canada, Vol. 1. 3rd edition. Toronto: McGraw Hill.

Watson, Patty J.
   1976   In pursuit of prehistoric subsistence: A comparative account of some contemporary flotation techniques. Midcontinental Journal of Archaeology, 1:77–100.

## TABLE 2.1
### Uncarbonized and Carbonized Seed and Plant Remains Identified from the Foxie Otter Site

| | |
|---|---|
| R1 | Hanks-A-1. Quadrant 1, Level 1. Concentration 112 cc, 24 g<br>**Uncarbonized seeds**—*Polygonum*[1] 1, *Prunus*[2] 1, *Sambucus* 1<br>**Needles**—*Thuja* |
| R2 | B-0-1, Fea. 1. Concentration 200 cc, 46 g<br>**Uncarbonized seeds**—unknown 4 |
| R3 | B-0-1, Fea.1. Concentrate 115 cc, 55 g<br>**Needles**—*Thuja* |
| R4 | B-0-3, Concentrate 700 cc, 123 g<br>**Uncarbonized seeds**—*Polygonum* 1, *Prunus* fragment, *Rubus* 1<br>**Fruit scale**—*Betula*<br>**Needles**—*Thuja* |
| R5 | B-0-3, depth 18 cm. Concentrate 100 cc, 27 g |
| R6 | B-0-3, Concentrate 95 cc, 67 g |
| R7 | B-0-3, Concentrate 135 cc, 15 g<br>**Uncarbonized seeds**—*Prunus* fragments<br>**Needles**—*Thuja* |
| R8 | B-0-3, Fea. 1. Concentrate 80 cc, 37 g<br>**Carbonized seed**—*Corylus* fragment |
| R9 | B-0-3, Fea. 1. Concentrate 100 cc, 37 g<br>**Uncarbonized seed**—*Prunus* 1 |
| R10 | B-0-4, Depth 13 cm. Concentrate 145 cc, 17 g |
| R11 | C-0-2, Concentrate 106 cc, 24 g<br>**Needles**—*Thuja* |
| R12 | E-0. Quadrant 4, Level 4. Concentrate 115 cc, 53 g<br>**Uncarbonized seed**—*Prunus* 1 |
| R13 | E-0. Hearth, Level 2. Concentrate 200 cc, 35 g<br>**Uncarbonized seeds**—*Betula* 1, *Rubus* 2, unknown 3<br>**Carbonized seeds**—*Rubus* 1 |
| R14 | E-0. Quadrant 2, Level 4. Concentrate 95 cc, 38 g<br>**Uncarbonized seeds**—*Prunus* 1<br>**Carbonized seeds**—*Corylus* 1 (frag.)<br>**Needles**—conifer fragments<br>**Artifact**—chert flake |

[1] *P.* cf *cilinode*
[2] *P. pensylvanica*

SOIL SAMPLES AND BOTANICAL SPECIMENS ARE HOUSED IN THE BOTANY DEPARTMENT, CANADIANA BUILDING, ROYAL ONTARIO MUSEUM IN TORONTO.

Botanical Lexicon: *Betula* = birch, *Corylus* = hazelnut, *Polygonum* = knotweed, *Prunus* = pin cherry, *Rubus* = raspberry, *Sambucus* = elderberry, *Thuja* = cedar, *Viola* = violet, *Picea* = spruce.

## Appendix 2

R15   Two lithic core fragments

R16   E-0. Hearth, Quadrant 3, Level 1. Concentrate 100 cc, 33 g
      **Uncarbonized seeds**—*Betula* 3, unknown 2

R17   E-00. Feature 3, Hearth, Quadrant 1, Level 3. Concentrate 500 cc, 56 g
      **Uncarbonized seeds**—*Prunus* 66

R18   E-0. Quadrant 2, Level 2. Concentrate 165 cc, 66 g
      **Uncarbonized seeds**—*Polygonum* 1
      **Needles**—*Picea*

R19   E-0. Quadrant ?, Level 3. Concentrate 90 cc, 29 g
      **Carbonized seed**—unknown 1

R20   E-0. Level 1. Concentrate 70 cc, 36 g
      **Fruit scale**—*Betula*

R21   38° 2N0W-2. Concentrate 70 cc, 36 g
      **Uncarbonized seeds**—*Viola*? 1
      **Needles**—*Thuja*

R22   7N0E. Quadrant 2, Level 2. Concentrate 210 cc, 94 g
      **Uncarbonized seeds**—*Betula* 1, *Prunus* 1, *Sambucus* 1
      **Artifacts**—quartz flake.

R23   E7N0E. Quadrant 3. Concentrate 120 cc, 45 g
      **Carbonized seeds**—*Sambucus* 1
      **Needles**—*Thuja*

R24   E7N0E. Quadrant 3, Level 3. Concentrate 130 cc, 75 g

R25   E8N0E. Quadrant 2, Level 2. Concentrate 84 cc, 42 g
      **Uncarbonized seeds**—*Thuja* 1
      **Needles**—*Thuja*

R26   E8N0E. Quadrant 4, Level 1. Concentrate 101 cc, 32 g
      **Uncarbonized seeds**—*Rubus* 1
      **Needles**—*Thuja*
      **Artifacts**—quartz flake

R27   E9N0E. Quadrant 2, Level 2. Concentrate 155 cc, 72 g
      **Uncarbonized seeds**—*Prunus* 1.
      **Fruit scale**—*Betula*
      **Needles**—*Picea, Thuja*
      **Cone scale**—*Thuja*
      **Artifacts**—chert flake

R28   E9N0E. Quadrant 3, Level 2. Concentrate 150 cc, 76 g
      **Carbonized seeds**—*Prunus* 1

R29  E9N0E. Quadrant 2, Level 2. Concentrate 175 cc, 104 g
**Uncarbonized seeds**—*Thuja*
**Needles**—*Thuja* 9

R30  9N2W. Quadrant 3, Level 2. Concentrate 175 cc, 20 g
**Uncarbonized seeds**—*Betula* 1, *Polygonum* 3, *Prunus* fragments, *Rubus* 7, *Viola*? 43, unknown 3

R31  9N2W. Quadrant 3, Level 2. Concentrate 50 cc, 4 g
**Uncarbonized seeds**—*Prunus* 1, *Rubus* 1, *Viola* 5

R32  38° 10N3W. Quadrant ?, Level 2. Concentrate 33 cc, 15 g

R33  38° 10N3W. Quadrant 3, Level 2. Concentrate 33 cc, 15 g

R34  38° 10N3W. Quadrant 3, Level 2. Concentrate 125 cc, 29 g
**Uncarbonized seeds**—*Prunus* fragments, *Rubus* 8, unknown 1

R35  38° 10N4W. Quadrant 3, Level 2. Concentrate 50 cc, 6 g

R36  38° 14N0W. Level 2. Concentrate 250 cc, 50 g
**Uncarbonized seeds**—*Betula* 2, *Prunus* 1, unknown 6

R37  38° 14N0W-2. Hearth, Level 2. Concentrate 225 cc, 143 g
Plant remains absent

R38  38° 14N0W-2. Feature 6, Level 2. Concentrate 175 cc, 108 g
**Uncarbonized seeds**—*Prunus* fragments
**Needles**—conifer fragments

R39  38° 14N0W-3. Concentrate 180 cc, 95 g
**Uncarbonized seeds**—*Prunus* fragments
**Needles**—*Picea*

R40  38° 14N0W-3. Level 2. Concentrate 175 cc, 108 g
**Carbonized seeds**—*Sambucus* 1

R41  38° 14N0W-3. Level 2. Concentrate 140 cc, 100 g

R42  38° 14N0w-3. Concentrate 140 cc, 100 g
**Carbonized seeds**—*Prunus* fragments, unknown 1.
**Fruit scale**—*Betula*
**Needles**—*Picea*

R43  38° 15N1W-1. Feature 8. Level 2. Concentrate 155 cc, 115 g
**Needles**—*Picea*

R44  38° 15N1W-1. Feature 3. Concentrate 80 cc, 70 g
Plant remains absent

R45  E0NE0. Quadrant 2, (extension 1). Concentrate 83 cc, 51 g
**Artifacts**—quartz flake.

---

Botanical Lexicon: *Betula* = birch, *Corylus* = hazelnut, *Polygonum* = knotweed, *Prunus* = pin cherry, *Rubus* = raspberry, *Sambucus* = elderberry, *Thuja* = cedar, *Viola* = violet, *Picea* = spruce.

*Appendix 2*

R46  E0NE0. Quadrant 2, (extension 2), Level 3. Concentrate 83 cc, 51 g
     **Artifacts**—chert flake, quartz flake

R47  E0NE0. Level 2. Concentrate 700 cc, 134 g
     **Carbonized seeds**—*Betula* 4, *Prunus* 1, *Rubus* 1, unknown 2
     **Needles**—*Thuja*. Cone scale—*Thuja*

R48  E0NE0. Quadrant 1, Level 2. Concentrate 285 cc, 47 g

R49  E0NE0. Quadrant 2, Level 3. Concentrate 200 cc, 16 g

R50  E0NE0. Quadrant 3, Level 3. Concentrate 100 cc, 77 g
     **Fruit scale**—*Betula*

R51  E0NE0. Feature 4. Quadrant 4, Level 2. Concentrate 190 cc, 47 g
     **Carbonized seeds**—*Prunus* 1

R52  O.S. 0NE0. Feature 7. Quadrant 2, Level 3. Concentrate 130 cc, 58 g
     Plant remains absent
     **Artifacts**—chert flake.

R53  O.S. 0NE0. Feature 7. Quadrant 2, Level 3. Concentrate 130 cc, 65 g
     Plant remains absent

R54  E. 0SE0-1. Concentrate 82 cc, 46g

R55  E. 0SE0-1. Concentrate 220 cc, 70 g
     **Fruit scale**—*Betula*
     **Needles**—*Picea*, *Thuja*

R56  E. 0SE0-2. Concentrate 185 cc, 63 g
     **Uncarbonized seeds**—*Betula* 1, *Prunus* 1
     **Needles**—*Thuja*

R57  E. 0SE0-2. Concentrate 400 cc, 51 g
     **Uncarbonized seeds**—*Betula* 1, *Prunus* 1, unknown 1
     **Carbonized seeds**—unknown 2

R58  Soil sample, comparative. Concentrate 165 cc, 63 g
     **Uncarbonized seeds**—*Betula* 1, *Prunus* fragments, *Rubus* 3
     **Needles**—*Picea*, *Thuja*

R59  Soil Sample, comparative. Concentrate 145 cc, 36 g
     **Uncarbonized seeds**—*Betula* 1, *Prunus* 1

R60  Soil sample, comparative. Concentrate 228 cc, 63 g
     **Uncarbonized seeds**—*Corylus* fragments

R61  Soil sample, comparative. Concentrate 238 cc, 81 g
     **Uncarbonized seeds**—*Betula* 1, *Thuja* 1
     **Needles**—*Picea*, *Thuja*
     **Cone scale**—*Thuja*

R62 Soil sample, comparative. Concentrate 40 cc, 26 g
**Uncarbonized seeds**—*Thuja* 1.
**Fruit scale**—*Betula*
**Needles**—*Picea, Thuja*

R63 Soil sample, comparative. Concentrate 50 cc, 10 g

R64 Soil sample, comparative. Concentrate 65 cc, 45 g
**Uncarbonized seeds**—*Prunus* fragments

R65 Soil sample, comparative. Concentrate 70 cc, 46g

R66 E. 1N0E-4. Concentrate 270 cc, 42 g
**Uncarbonized seeds**—*Prunus* fragments
**Carbonized seeds**—unknown 1

R67 E.1N0E-2. Concentrate 200 cc, 75 g
**Fruit scale**—*Betula*
**Needles**—*Picea, Thuja*?
**Artifacts**—chert flake, quartz flake

R68 E. 1N0E-4. Hearth. Concentrate 105 cc, 42 g
**Needles**—*Thuja*
**Artifacts**—chert flake

R69 No provenience on bag.

---

Botanical Lexicon: *Betula* = birch, *Corylus* = hazelnut, *Polygonum* = knotweed, *Prunus* = pin cherry, *Rubus* = raspberry, *Sambucus* = elderberry, *Thuja* = cedar, *Viola* = violet, *Picea* = spruce.

## Appendix 2

### TABLE 2.2
### Carbonized Wood (>5mm) in Grams from Foxie Otter Site

| ROM #[a] | Acer[b] | Betula[c] | Populus/ Salix[d] | I.D.P.[e] | I[f] | Pinus[g] | I.C.[h] | Total |
|---|---|---|---|---|---|---|---|---|
| 3 | - | - | - | - | - | .1 | .1 | .2 |
| 4 | - | - | - | - | - | - | .2 | .2 |
| 5 | - | - | - | - | - | .1 | .3 | .4 |
| 9 | - | - | - | - | - | .3 | - | .3 |
| 11 | - | - | - | .1 | - | - | - | .1 |
| 12 | - | - | - | - | - | .1 | .2 | .3 |
| 17 | - | - | - | - | .9 | 2.8 | .8 | 4.5 |
| 18 | - | - | - | - | - | 1.4 | .9 | 2.3 |
| 20 | - | - | - | - | - | - | 1.3 | 1.3 |
| 22 | .3 | - | - | .1 | - | .2 | .1 | .7 |
| 23 | - | - | - | - | .1 | .9 | .1 | 1.1 |
| 24 | - | - | - | - | - | - | .1 | .1 |
| 25 | - | - | - | - | - | .2 | .1 | .3 |
| 27 | - | - | - | - | - | .2 | .1 | .3 |
| 28 | .1 | - | - | - | - | .1 | .1 | .3 |
| 30 | - | - | - | - | .1 | .1 | .1 | .3 |
| 31 | - | - | - | - | .1 | - | .1 | .2 |
| 33 | - | .1 | - | - | .1 | - | .1 | .3 |
| 34 | - | - | - | - | - | .1 | .2 | .3 |
| 35 | - | - | - | - | - | .2 | .1 | .3 |
| 36 | - | - | - | - | - | .1 | .2 | .3 |
| 40 | - | - | - | - | - | - | .1 | .1 |
| 41 | - | - | - | - | - | .1 | .1 | .2 |
| 43 | - | - | - | - | - | 1.0 | - | 1.0 |
| 46 | - | - | - | .3 | - | - | - | .3 |
| 47 | - | - | .9 | .1 | - | .2 | .3 | 1.5 |
| 48 | - | - | 1.8 | .2 | .3 | .5 | .2 | 3.0 |
| 51 | - | - | .7 | .1 | - | .2 | .1 | 1.1 |
| 53 | - | - | .1 | - | - | .1 | .1 | .3 |
| 54 | - | - | - | - | .2 | - | .3 | .5 |
| 55 | - | - | .1 | .2 | .1 | - | .1 | .5 |
| 56 | - | - | .4 | .1 | .1 | .1 | .1 | .8 |
| 57 | - | - | 1.0 | .1 | .1 | .1 | .2 | 1.5 |
| 59 | - | - | - | - | - | .1 | .1 | .2 |
| 65 | - | - | - | - | - | .1 | .1 | .2 |
| 66 | - | - | - | - | - | 1.7 | .3 | 2.0 |
| 67 | - | - | - | - | - | 7.2 | .3 | 7.5 |
| 68 | - | .1 | - | .2 | - | .6 | .3 | 1.2 |
| Total | .4 | .2 | 5.0 | 1.5 | 2.1 | 18.9 | 7.9 | 36.0 |
| % | 1.1 | .6 | 13.8 | 4.2 | 5.8 | 52.5 | 21.9 | 99.9 |

[a]Royal Ontario Museum catalog number
[b]Maple
[c]Birch
[d]Poplar/Willow
[e]Indeterminable diffuse porous
[f]Indeterminable
[g]Pine
[h]Indeterminable conifer

# Appendix 3
## SAMPLE OF DATA SUBMITTED TO SIMON FRASER UNIVERSITY RADIOCARBON LABORATORY

The submitted samples were charcoal from site CdHk-3, located at 46° 36' 45" N. latitude/81° 43' 45" W. longitude/el. 339 m above sea level. References to pertinent published information can be found in "Archaeology of the Spanish River," by C. Hanks (1981), on file with the Ontario Heritage Foundation.

**Sample # 1717**

**Location of sample:** CdHk-3, Sq. O.S. 0S0E, Quad 1, Level 3. Top of the orange lacustrine clay, thought to date a Woodland component.

**Significance:** Dates the base of the culture-bearing gray podzol layer.

**Estimated age:** A.D. 700—A.D. 1300

**Calculated age:** 1840 ± 350 B.P.

**Sample # 169**

**Location of sample:** Site CdHk-3, Sq. O.S. 0N0E, Quad. 2, Level 3, Feature 7. A possible hearth feature in the podzol layer.

**Sigificance:** Feature 7 is thought to relate to a Woodland period occupation.

**Estimated age:** A.D. 750—A.D. 1300

**Calculated age:** 480 ± 260 B.P.

**Sample # 170**

**Location of sample:** Site CdHk-3, Sq 38°14N0W, Quad 2, Level 2, Feature 6. Gray podzol layer in association with dense cluster of reduction flakes.

**Significance:** This dates a feature consisting of reduction flakes made of graywacke. It is the second date on an activity area that was previously dated in 1980 at 7670 ± 120 B.P.[1] on 40 g of charcoal. Because of the small size of this sample and the large standard deviation in comparison to the first date, the integrity of this sample is questionable.

---

[1]Processed by Teledyne, cited in Hanks 1981.

**Estimated age:** 7000 B.P.

**Calculated age:** 1320 ± 700 B.P.

---

**Sample # 155**

**Location of sample:** CdHk-3, Sq. Sc. E. 0N0E, Quad. 1, Level 2, Feature 4. Gray podzol layer, dates lower layers of a hearth with a probable Late Woodland association.

**Significance:** Dates an archaeological feature believed to have a Late Woodland association.

**Estimated age:** A.D. 700—A.D. 1300.

**Calculated age:** 1450 ± 250 B.P.

---

**Sample # 154**

**Location of sample:** CdHk-3, Sq. E-0, Quad. 4, Level 4. A portion of a hearth contained in a podzol lens slumped in an eroding lake bank.

**Significance:** A hearth feature in association with a single body sherd of grit-tempered ceramics. A Woodland period date is expected.

**Estimated age:** A.D. 700—A.D. 1300.

**Calculated age:** 610 ± 80 B.P.

---

**Sample # 153**

**Location of sample:** CdHk-3, Sq. Sc. E. 0S0E, Quad. 2, Level 2, Feature 4. Top portion of hearth feature in podzol.

**Significance:** Part of an archaeological feature thought to be a hearth of Woodland origin.

**Estimated age:** A.D. 700—A.D. 1300.

**Calculated age:** 370 ± 90 B.P.

---

**Sample # 152**

**Location of sample:** CdHk-3, Sq. Sc. E. 1N0E, Quad 3, Level 2, podzol.

**Significance:** This sample was thought to date the base of the podzol culture-bearing layer. The late date and the large standard deviation make that unlikely.

**Estimated age:** A.D. 700—A.D. 1300.

**Calculated age:** 170 ± 120 B.P.

---

**Sample # 151**

**Location of sample:** CdHk-3, Sq. Sc. E. 0N0E, Quad. 4, Level 2, Feature 4. Gray podzol.

**Significance:** Sample from a hearth believed to be from the Woodland period.

**Estimated age:** A.D. 700—A.D. 1300

**Calculated age:** 690 ± 180 B.P.

# Appendix 4
# RESIDUE ANALYSIS OF FOXIE OTTER SITE CHIPPED STONE

*by*
*Michael Broderick*

## PART 1. Residue Analysis of Stone Tools

### Introduction

In recent years, archaeologists have studied microwear patterns on artifacts to determine how they were used and to infer the materials they were used on (e.g. Frison 1968; Hayden 1979; Hester et al. 1973; Keeley 1974, 1980; Nance 1970, 1971; Odell 1980; Semonov 1964; Singer and Gibson 1970; Wilmsen 1970). More recently, workers have been attempting to isolate and identify residual chemicals and tissue fragments from artifacts which are believed to be associated with the plants and animals the tools were used on. Bruier (1976) used chemical reagents, and Schaffer and Holloway (1979) used microscopy to identify residual plant and animal matter from artifacts recovered from dry sites in the American Southwest, while the use of paper chromatography on an artifact from Hope, British Columbia, demonstrated the persistence of amino acids presumed to be associated with the organisms the tool was used on (Broderick 1979). In this case the artifacts were exposed to a wet environment, and it is apparent that the persistence of residues was not affected by leaching due to rainfall.

Further work in the field of residue analysis indicates that it is possible to identify broad classes of biochemical materials such as blood, fat, starch, and resin from hygric sites with variable soil pH values (Broderick n.d.). Artifacts used in this study were recovered from the Crescent Beach site (DgRr-1), a shell midden with a high soil pH, and the Pitt River site (DhRq-21), a riverine site with a low soil pH. This study also suggests that it is possible to deduce how the tools were used through the identification of regions on artifact surfaces which have variable concentrations of residues.

The fundamental hypothesis underlying studies of this nature is that if an artifact has been used on plant or animal tissue for a period of time, then one might expect a transfer of matter to the surface of the tool which would persist as a residue. Although the works cited above demonstrate that the potential of this hypothesis being true is high, it has yet to be formally experimentally tested. Experimental controls thus far have been negative tests where tools tested in the same manner as their surrounding soil matrices have yielded different results. Experimental work aimed at demonstrating the validity of this hypothesis is continuing, and results are encouraging. For the present time, however, speculation will continue.

This report concerns the analysis of residues removed from a number of tools recovered from the Foxie Otter site in response to a request by Christopher Hanks. The site is located in northern Ontario, and Hanks informed me that the tools from this site have considerable antiquity (ca. 7000 B.P.).

Three chemical spot tests were used to determine whether blood, starch, fat, or resin were present as a residue on the artifact surfaces. The results were used to hypothesize whether the tools were used on plant or animal tissue, and how the tools were used, by identifying variation in the types of residue deposited at different regions of the tool surfaces. The results of this study may be used in conjunction with edge wear studies and other more conventional methods to better determine tool use.

Three chemical reagents were used for spot tests in this analysis: benzidine (4–4′ diamino biphenyl) was used to test for the presence of blood; Sudan III (tetrazobenzine-B-naphthol) was used to determine the presence of fat and resin, and potassium iodide (KI) was used to detect starch. Blood and fat residues on a tool suggest that the tool was used on animal tissue, and starch implies it was used on plant tissue. Resin may either indicate use on wood, or it may have been used as a fixative as an aid to hafting. The method of obtaining samples from artifacts is described below, as well as a detailed description of each spot test. Results are presented on an artifact form containing a drawing of the artifact on a reference grid showing the sample loci, and the test results are indicated in a positive or negative fashion on a table. A discussion of the results follows each artifact.

## Methods

### The Removal of Sample

Samples were obtained by probing artifact surfaces in various locations with a dissecting needle and removing 5–10 mg samples of the artifact surface and depositing them on a clean microscope slide. The needle was sterilized after work at each locus by heating it to red-hot in a flame and quenching it in methanol to maintain its hardness. The locations of the samples were indicated on outline drawings of each artifact on the artifact forms included in the results. Different loci on each artifact were sampled, as it was anticipated that variation in the types of residue at different locations on the tool may provide information on how the tool was used. Damage to tools resulting from this technique was limited to small scratches on the surface, and in most cases, these scratches are not noticeable to the naked eye. All sampling was carried out under a microscope ($9 \times$ magnification).

### The Benzidine Test

The compound benzidine (4–4′ diamino biphenyl) is used routinely as a reagent to detect blood in criminal investigations, and has a reported sensitivity of $2 \times 10^{-6}$ parts blood (Hawk et al. 1948:434). A slurry of benzidine and glacial acetic acid ($CH_3COOH$) was prepared (approximately 50 mg

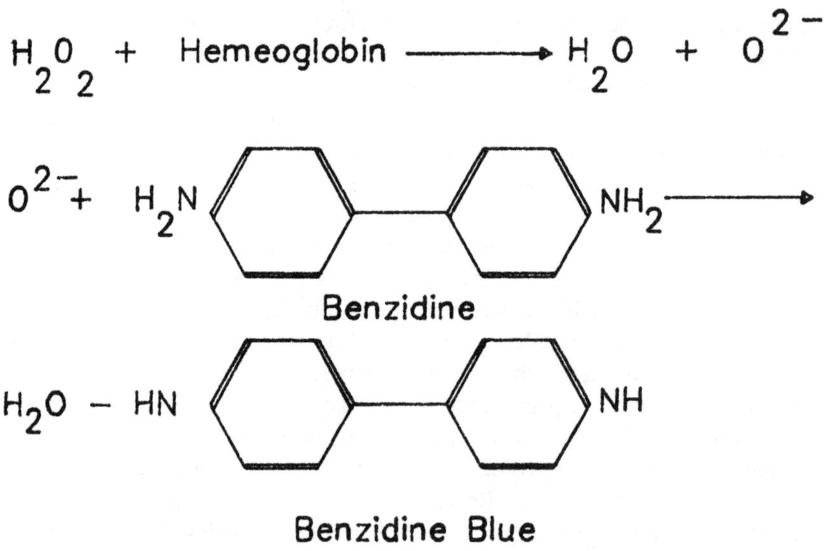

$H_2O_2$ + Hemeoglobin ⟶ $H_2O$ + $O^{2-}$

$O^{2-}$ + $H_2N$—⟨ ⟩—⟨ ⟩—$NH_2$ ⟶

Benzidine

$H_2O$ − HN=⟨ ⟩—⟨ ⟩=NH

Benzidine Blue

Figure 4.1 Rearrangement of the bonding of the benzidine molecule (after Fiegl 1966:188).

benzidine to 0.25 ml acetic acid) and a drop was placed on an artifact sample so that the particles of the sample would mix with the slurry. A drop of 30% hydrogen peroxide ($H_2O_2$) was added, and if blood residue was present, blue color would form in the slurry within 30 seconds. Hawk (1947:438) explains that hemoglobin in blood reacts with the hydrogen peroxide forming a molecule of water and a liberated oxygen atom ($O^{2-}$). The oxygen then combines with the benzidine molecule, turning it blue. Feigl (1966:188) points out that the formation of the blue color results from a rearrangement of the bonding of the benzidine molecule brought about by the loss of a hydrogen molecule from each amine group ($NH_2$) of the molecule. This rearrangement is diagrammed in Figure 4.1.

The use of the benzidine test was first described to me by Mr. E. J. Fennell of the Vancouver City Analyst's Laboratory, who, until the time of his retirement, used the test routinely for the preliminary identification of blood in criminal investigations. Fennell informed me, however, that the test also reacts with peroxidases present in fresh fruits and vegetables, and for this reason, evidence based on this test alone is insufficient to be accepted in Canadian criminal courts. This is not a concern in archaeology, however, as plant peroxidases are short-lived.

## The Sudan III Test for Fat and Resin

Sudan III (tetrazobenzine–B–naphthol) is a common histological stain specific to the fatty acids that are found in fats and marbled throughout resins (Johansen 1940:63), and its use was suggested to me by M. Florian of the British Columbia Provincial Museum. A 0.9% solution of Sudan III and methanol was prepared, and a drop was applied to a residue sample while being observed under a dissecting microscope (9 × magnification), and the entire sample was observed to change to an orange color. The sample was then flushed with a drop of pure methanol, and resin in the sample would remain stained while other particles in the sample would clear. Particles of resin were found to be notably pliable and ductile, and their identification could be verified by rolling them flat with the dissecting needle.

Fats in the residue sample were dissolved in the methanol Sudan III solvent. As the solvent front advanced from the point of application, dissolved fats precipitated in an amber ring behind the maximum advance of the solvent front. The mechanism for this appears to be chromatographic in the sense that the stain molecules attach to the fat molecules and "weigh them down" so that their mobility across the slide is impaired in relation to the solvent front. This is illustrated in Figure 4.2.

Resins exude from secretory ducts in gymnosperm leaves, xylem, and phloem (Esau 1953:69, 292, 249). They contain oils and fats (Parry et al. 1925:219) which are the components that bind to the Sudan III (Johansen 1940:64). Fats are non-water soluble lipids composed of fatty acids and glycerol and are found in both plants and animals, although they are more common in animals (Hawks et. al. 1948:86–92).

## The Iodide Test for Starch

When the aqueous iodide anion ($I^-$) obtained from dissolving potassium iodide (KI) contacts starch, an iodine-starch complex is formed and a blue-black color results. This reaction, known since 1814 (Pearse 1961:4), is not entirely understood. Hawk (1948:76) ventures that a compound is not formed, but rather, the color results as an absorption complex. The test is used here to detect the presence of starch in residue samples, thus showing whether tools had been used on plant tissue. Starch is a product of photosynthesis and appears in many plant organs, particularly storage organs such as tubers and corms (Esau 1953:28). Generally, starch contains about 20% of a water soluble fraction known as amylose, and about 80% of a water insoluble fraction amylopectin (Morrison and Boyd 1967:1027). It is suspected that the latter fraction would persist on archaeological tools, as its water insolubility would foster longevity in the archaeological record.

A 1% solution of potassium iodide and methanol was prepared, and a drop applied to the sample while being observed under a microscope. Starch was

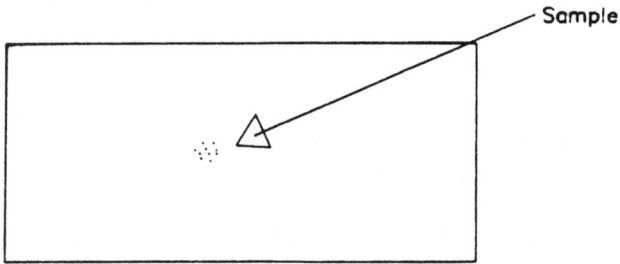

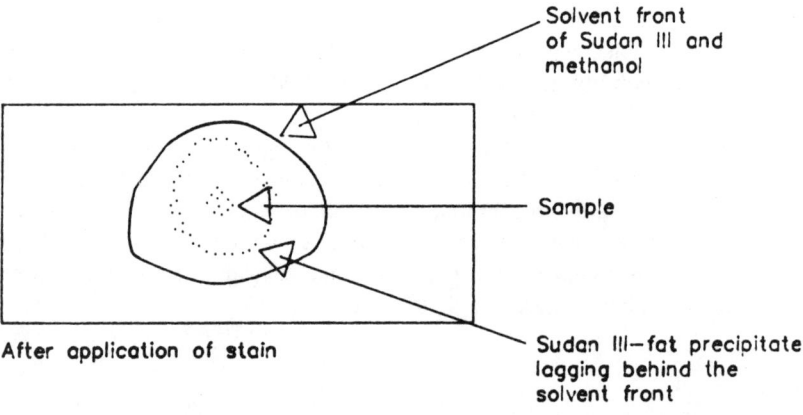

Figure 4.2. A residue sample containing fat before and after the application of the Sudan III stain.

indicated if a blue-black color was apparent either at the point of application or in the solvent front.

*Interpretation*

The results of residue analysis were evaluated in the following manner. If blood was present as identified by the benzidine test, then use on animal tissue was inferred, because, though fat occurs in plants, it is much more abundant in animal tissue. There is a strong possibility that if fat is found in the absence of blood residue, that the tool may have been used on cooked flesh. I have conducted preliminary experiments on modern flakes, finding

## Appendix 4

that the potential of blood persistence on an artifact is drastically reduced if the flesh was cooked. The presence of starch indicates that the tool was either used on wood, or that resin in the form of pitch was used as an aid to the manufacture or use of the tool (i.e., a fixative as an aid to hafting).

An attempt was made to evaluate the method of tool use of some of the artifacts by examining different locations of the artifact surfaces and noting the results at each location. Special attention was devoted to locating regions of different concentration and types of residues in the hopes that this differentiation might allow speculation on whether the tool was used as a knife or scraper, for example. Such information might be of value in forming scenarios concerning the activities of the archaeological site.

## Results

Following are the results of residue analysis performed on a number of artifacts from the Foxie Otter site. Test results for each artifact are presented, including the artifact number, a scaled outline drawing of the artifact indicating locations of the samples, and a table showing the results of tests in a positive or negative fashion. A discussion of each artifact is given after the table. Summary and conclusion are given on page 147.

**ARTIFACT RESIDUE ANALYSIS FORM**      Artifact # __34___

Sample Locations

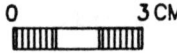

Results:

| Locus | Grid Location (x,y) | Blood | Fat | Resin | Starch |
|---|---|---|---|---|---|
| 1 | (15.4, 10.0) | + | − | + | − |
| 2 | (15.4, 10.4) | + | + | + | + |
| 3 | (15.3, 11.2) | − | + | + | − |
| 4 | (17.8, 9.5) | + | + | + | + |
| 5 | (18.4, 10.2) | + | + | + | + |

**Artifact 34.** This tool showed all of the residues at 3 of the 5 loci examined, indicating that it had been used in some fashion on both plant and animal tissue. Owing to its small size, it appears that this tool is a fragment of a larger one. Perhaps it is a resharpening flake.

*Appendix 4*                                                                107

## ARTIFACT RESIDUE ANALYSIS FORM                    Artifact # __75____
Sample Locations

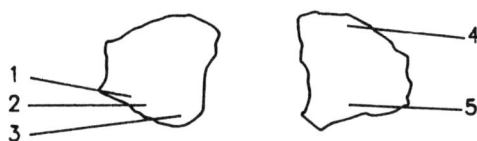

Results:

| Locus | Grid Location (x,y) | Blood | Fat | Resin | Starch |
|---|---|---|---|---|---|
| 1 | (12.0, 10.0) | − | − | + | − |
| 2 | (12.7, 10.4) | − | − | + | − |
| 3 | (14.2, 10.7) | − | − | + | − |
| 4 | (21.2, 7.1) | + | + | − | − |
| 5 | (21.4, 10.4) | − | − | + | − |

**Artifact 75.** This tool was examined at 5 loci, and resin was identified along the steep edge at loci 1, 3, 4, and 5. Blood and fat were located at the opposite edge. It appears from this that the tool was used on animal tissue, and that the resin deposits likely indicate some form of hafting.

*Foxie Otter Site*

**ARTIFACT RESIDUE ANALYSIS FORM**          Artifact # __78__

Sample Locations

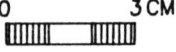

Results:

| Locus | Grid Location (x,y) | Blood | Fat | Resin | Starch |
|---|---|---|---|---|---|
| 1 | (15.4, 11.0) | – | – | – | – |
| 2 | (16.5, 11.5) | – | – | – | – |

**Artifact 78.** This artifact was examined at 2 loci and no residues were found.

*Appendix 4*

## ARTIFACT RESIDUE ANALYSIS FORM

Artifact # __83__

Sample Locations

0          3 CM

Results:

| Locus | Grid Location (x,y) | Blood | Fat | Resin | Starch |
|-------|---------------------|-------|-----|-------|--------|
| 1 | (16.6, 11.0) | – | – | – | – |
| 2 | (22.6, 10.4) | – | – | – | – |

**Artifact 83.** This tool was examined at 2 loci and no residues were found.

**ARTIFACT RESIDUE ANALYSIS FORM**          Artifact # __134__

Sample Locations

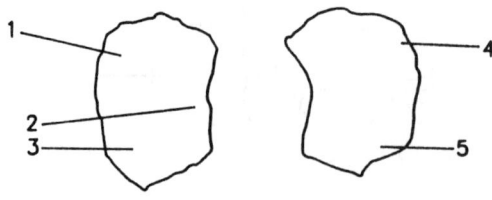

Results:

| Locus | Grid Location (x,y) | Blood | Fat | Resin | Starch |
|-------|---------------------|-------|-----|-------|--------|
| 1 | (12.0, 10.0) | + | + | − | − |
| 2 | (15.0, 12.0) | − | + | − | − |
| 3 | (12.5, 13.6) | + | + | − | − |
| 4 | (9.4, 23.5) | + | + | − | − |
| 5 | (22.6, 13.5) | + | + | − | − |

**Artifact 134.** This tool was examined at 5 loci, and blood and fat were recovered at all but locus 2 on the cortex, which contained only fat. It is apparent that the tool was used on animal tissue. It is also evident that the cortex was not in direct contact with the tissue as blood was absent. It is possible that this tool was either hand-held or hafted at the cortex, as this might offer some protection from the blood residue. The tool may be a scraper.

## ARTIFACT RESIDUE ANALYSIS FORM

Artifact # __149__

Sample Locations

Results:

| Locus | Grid Location (x,y) | Blood | Fat | Resin | Starch |
|---|---|---|---|---|---|
| 1 | (20.7, 8.6) | + | + | – | – |
| 2 | (19.8, 9.7) | + | + | – | – |
| 3 | (20.6, 8.2) | – | – | – | – |

**Artifact 149.** This tool was examined at 3 loci and blood and fat were recovered at all but locus 3 which was located on the steep edge. The tool was apparently used on animal tissue, and the absence of residue on the steep edge may indicate that the tool was a fragment of a larger tool that was either broken through use, or flaked off during resharpening.

## ARTIFACT RESIDUE ANALYSIS FORM

Artifact # __156__

Sample Locations

0         3 CM

**Results:**

| Locus | Grid Location (x,y) | Blood | Fat | Resin | Starch |
|---|---|---|---|---|---|
| 1 | (11.6, 8.6) | + | + | − | − |
| 2 | (11.4, 10.7) | − | + | − | − |
| 3 | (21.7, 8.8) | + | + | − | − |
| 4 | (17.6, 10.0) | − | + | − | − |
| 5 | (19.3, 11.4) | − | − | − | − |

**Artifact 156.** This tool was examined at 5 locations and all but locus 5 showed evidence that it had been used on animal tissue. The artifact may have been used as a hand-held knife in cutting animal tissue.

*Appendix 4*

**ARTIFACT RESIDUE ANALYSIS FORM**  Artifact # 162

Sample Locations

0　　　3CM

**Results:**

| Locus | Grid Location (x,y) | Blood | Fat | Resin | Starch |
|---|---|---|---|---|---|
| 1 | (10.4, 12.4) | – | – | – | – |

**Artifact 162.** This artifact was examined at 1 locus and no residues were found.

*114*  *Foxie Otter Site*

**ARTIFACT RESIDUE ANALYSIS FORM**  Artifact # _163_
Sample Locations

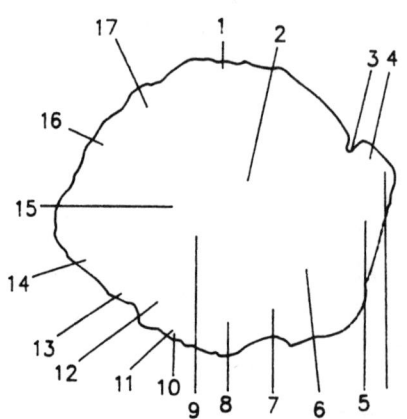
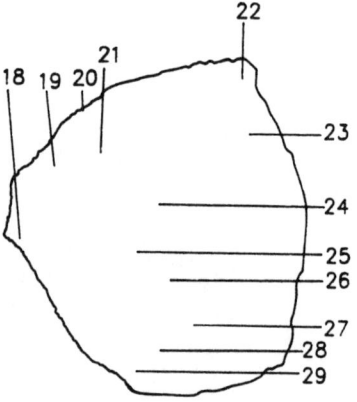

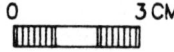

Results:

| Locus | Grid Location (x,y) | Blood | Fat | Resin | Starch |
|---|---|---|---|---|---|
| 1 | (9.5, 2.7) | + | + | – | – |
| 2 | (10.6, 7.4) | + | + | – | – |
| 3 | (15.0, 6.0) | + | + | + | – |
| 4 | (15.7, 6.4) | – | – | + | – |
| 5 | (16.4, 7.0) | – | – | + | – |
| 6 | (15.6, 9.0) | – | – | + | – |
| 7 | (13.0, 11.0) | + | + | + | – |
| 8 | (11.7, 12.6) | – | + | – | – |
| 9 | (9.8, 13.2) | + | + | – | – |
| 10 | (8.4, 9.6) | + | + | – | – |
| 11 | (13.5, 7.4) | + | + | – | – |
| 12 | (6.7, 12.3) | + | + | – | – |
| 13 | (5.2, 12.0) | + | + | – | – |
| 14 | (3.7, 10.7) | + | + | – | – |
| 15 | (7.4, 8.4) | + | + | – | – |
| 16 | (4.4, 5.8) | – | + | – | – |
| 17 | (6.3, 4.4) | – | + | – | – |
| 18 | (21.0, 10.0) | + | + | – | – |
| 19 | (22.5, 7.0) | + | + | – | – |
| 20 | (23.6, 4.6) | – | + | – | – |
| 21 | (24.4, 6.4) | – | + | – | – |
| 22 | (30.4, 3.4) | + | + | – | – |
| 23 | (30.9, 5.6) | – | + | – | – |
| 24 | (26.9, 8.5) | – | – | – | – |
| 25 | (26.0, 10.5) | – | – | – | – |
| 26 | (27.5, 11.6) | – | – | – | – |
| 27 | (28.5, 13.4) | – | – | – | – |
| 28 | (27.0, 14.5) | – | – | + | – |
| 29 | (26.0, 15.4) | – | – | + | – |

**Artifact 163.** This tool was examined at 29 loci and blood, fat, and resin residues were located. As resin residues were restricted to both sides of one region of the tool (loci 3, 4, 5, 6, 28, and 29), hafting is suspected. The left portion of this artifact is roughly flat, while the right portion is convex. The higher portions of the convex side (loci 24, 25, 26, and 27) are free of residue, while the other side has a more or less even distribution of blood and fat residues. Because of this difference in residue accumulation between the two sides, it is suggested that the left side of the tool was the one in the most frequent contact with flesh. The artifact likely functioned as a hafted scraper, perhaps used in the processing of hides.

*Foxie Otter Site*

**ARTIFACT RESIDUE ANALYSIS FORM**    Artifact # 164

Sample Locations

0        3 CM

**Results:**

| Locus | Grid Location (x,y) | Blood | Fat | Resin | Starch |
|---|---|---|---|---|---|
| 1 | (14.6, 8.6) | – | – | – | – |
| 2 | (13.8, 10.8) | – | – | + | – |
| 3 | (19.0, 8.6) | – | – | – | – |
| 4 | (19.4, 11.3) | – | – | + | – |

**Artifact 164.** This tool was examined at 4 loci, and only resin was found at loci 2 and 4 on the narrow portion of the artifact. It is possible that the tool was hafted at the narrow portion. Alternatively, the narrow portion of the tool may have been used for wood-working.

# ARTIFACT RESIDUE ANALYSIS FORM

Artifact # __171__

Sample Locations

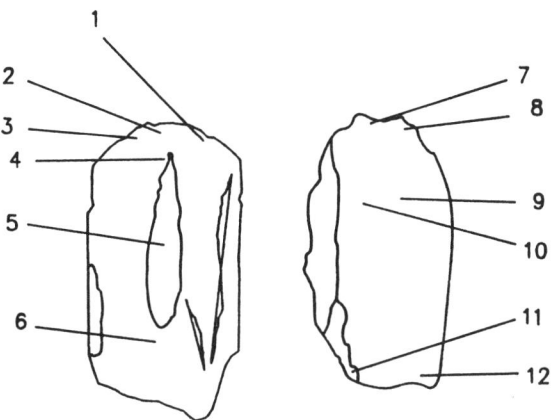

Results:

| Locus | Grid Location (x,y) | Blood | Fat | Resin | Starch |
|---|---|---|---|---|---|
| 1 | (13.5, 7.0) | − | − | + | − |
| 2 | (11.8, 6.6) | − | − | + | − |
| 3 | (10.8, 6.8) | − | − | + | − |
| 4 | (11.8, 7.6) | − | − | + | − |
| 5 | (11.9, 11.2) | − | − | − | − |
| 6 | (11.4, 15.0) | − | − | − | − |
| 7 | (20.5, 6.4) | − | − | + | − |
| 8 | (22.0, 6.5) | − | − | + | − |
| 9 | (20.4, 9.3) | − | − | + | − |
| 10 | (21.8, 9.5) | − | − | + | − |
| 11 | (19.6, 16.4) | − | − | − | − |
| 12 | (22.5, 16.5) | − | − | − | − |

**Artifact 171.** This tool was examined at 12 locations and resin was recovered at loci 1, 2, 3, 4, 7, 8, 9, and 10 along the steep edge of the tool. It should be commented that this residue was visible under 9× magnification, and some wood fragments are mixed with it. The tool was doubtless used for wood-working, likely as a plane or scraper.

## ARTIFACT RESIDUE ANALYSIS FORM

Artifact # __172__

Sample Locations

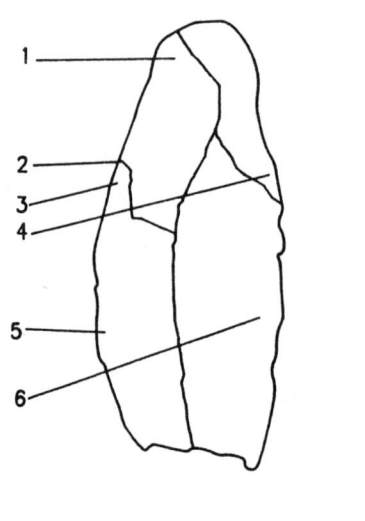
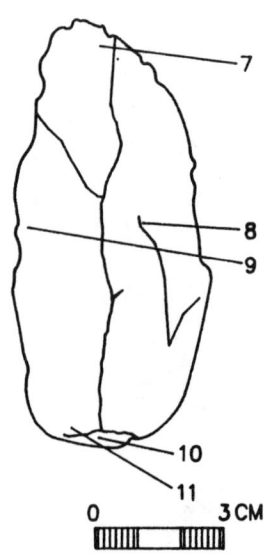

### Results:

| Locus | Grid Location (x,y) | Blood | Fat | Resin | Starch |
|-------|---------------------|-------|-----|-------|--------|
| 1  | (11.7, 3.7)  | – | – | + | – |
| 2  | (9.4, 7.8)   | – | – | + | – |
| 3  | (9.1, 8.6)   | – | – | + | – |
| 4  | (15.6, 8.4)  | – | – | + | – |
| 5  | (8.6, 14.7)  | – | – | + | – |
| 6  | (15.1, 14.2) | – | – | + | – |
| 7  | (21.4, 3.9)  | – | – | + | – |
| 8  | (26.2, 11.1) | – | – | + | – |
| 9  | (21.5, 11.3) | – | – | + | – |
| 10 | (24.4, 19.7) | – | – | – | – |
| 11 | (23.2, 19.3) | – | – | – | – |

**Artifact 172.** This tool was examined at 11 locations. Resin was found at all loci but 10 and 11. Due to the concentrations of resin at each locus, it is suspected that the tool was used on wood. There is no evidence of hafting at the basal region.

*Appendix 4*

## ARTIFACT RESIDUE ANALYSIS FORM

Artifact # 173

Sample Locations

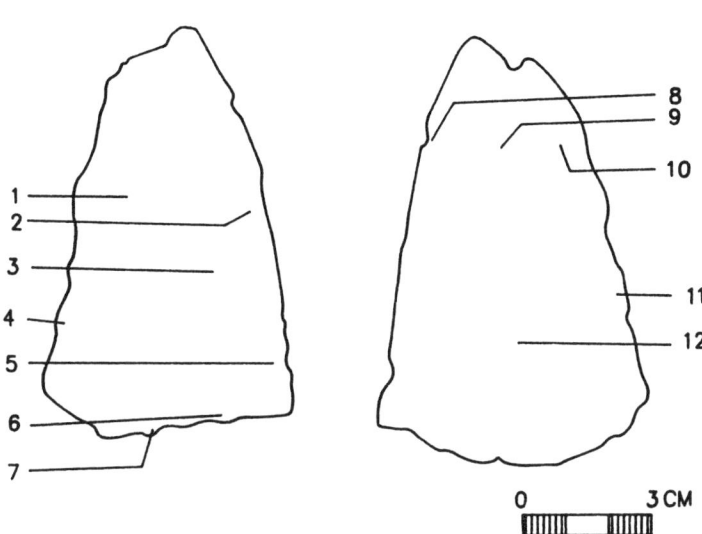

Results:

| Locus | Grid Location (x,y) | Blood | Fat | Resin | Starch |
|---|---|---|---|---|---|
| 1 | (7.6, 10.4) | − | + | − | − |
| 2 | (12.8, 11.0) | − | + | + | − |
| 3 | (11.2, 13.4) | + | + | + | − |
| 4 | (4.8, 15.5) | + | + | − | − |
| 5 | (13.6, 17.2) | − | − | + | − |
| 6 | (11.5, 19.4) | − | + | + | − |
| 7 | (8.6, 19.8) | − | + | + | − |
| 8 | (20.4, 8.2) | − | + | + | − |
| 9 | (23.4, 8.5) | + | + | + | − |
| 10 | (25.6, 8.4) | − | + | + | − |
| 11 | (28.0, 14.4) | − | + | + | − |
| 12 | (24.0, 16.1) | + | + | + | − |

**Artifact 173.** This tool was examined at 12 loci, and blood, fat, and resin residues were recovered indicating that the tool was used on both plant and animal tissue. Blood is the rarest residue, occurring at loci 3, 4, 9, and 12, which, with the exception of 12, are located away from the edge of the tool with a maximum accumulation near the center. This is the type of residue pattern one might expect of a tool that was used as a knife. The continued sawing action would cause a build-up of residue near the center of the tool. Thus, this tool was likely a multi-purpose knife.

## ARTIFACT RESIDUE ANALYSIS FORM

Artifact # __180__

Sample Locations

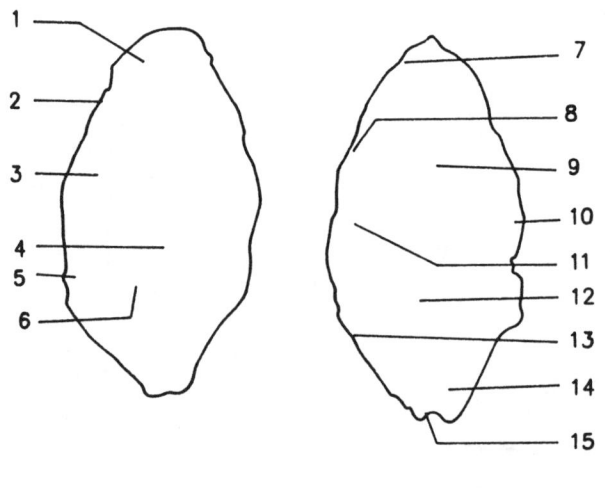

Results:

| Locus | Grid Location (x,y) | Blood | Fat | Resin | Starch |
|---|---|---|---|---|---|
| 1 | (10.9, 4.2) | + | + | − | − |
| 2 | (9.1, 5.7) | − | − | − | + |
| 3 | (8.8, 8.6) | + | + | − | − |
| 4 | (11.8, 11.6) | + | + | − | − |
| 5 | (8.0, 12.8) | + | + | − | + |
| 6 | (10.5, 13.2) | + | + | − | + |
| 7 | (21.7, 4.4) | + | + | − | − |
| 8 | (19.6, 7.8) | + | + | − | + |
| 9 | (23.1, 8.4) | + | + | − | + |
| 10 | (26.4, 10.8) | + | + | − | + |
| 11 | (19.6, 10.7) | + | + | − | + |
| 12 | (22.5, 13.7) | + | + | − | + |
| 13 | (19.6, 15.4) | − | − | − | − |
| 14 | (23.6, 17.4) | − | − | − | − |
| 15 | (22.6, 18.5) | − | − | − | − |

**Artifact 180.** This tool was examined at 15 loci and blood, fat, and starch residues were found indicating that the tool was used on both plant and animal matter. There was not sufficient differentiation of residues on the tool to determine whether it was used as a knife or a chopper. Both edges and sides exhibited residues of roughly equal proportions. The conspicuous absence of residue at the basal region of the tool (loci 13, 14, and 15) might indicate that this area was shielded from residues, likely by some form of haft. Resin was not used as a fixative in this case, as none was present as a residue.

*Appendix 4*

**ARTIFACT RESIDUE ANALYSIS FORM**     Artifact # __184__

Sample Locations

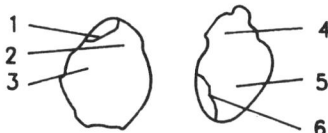

0　　3 CM

Results:

| Locus | Grid Location (x,y) | Blood | Fat | Resin | Starch |
|---|---|---|---|---|---|
| 1 | (15.0, 9.9) | + | + | − | − |
| 2 | (16.0, 10.1) | − | + | − | − |
| 3 | (14.5, 10.9) | + | + | − | − |
| 4 | (20.4, 9.6) | − | + | − | − |
| 5 | (20.6, 11.8) | − | + | − | − |
| 6 | (19.5, 12.2) | − | + | − | − |

**Artifact 184.** This tool was examined at 6 locations, and fat residue was found at each, with blood appearing at loci 1 and 3. No explanation of this differentiation is offered. It appears that this tool was used on animal tissue.

**ARTIFACT RESIDUE ANALYSIS FORM**                    Artifact # __186__

**Sample Locations**

0          3 CM

**Results:**

| Locus | Grid Location (x,y) | Blood | Fat | Resin | Starch |
|---|---|---|---|---|---|
| 1 | (13.4, 8.6) | − | + | + | − |
| 2 | (14.2, 10.8) | − | + | + | − |
| 3 | (14.1, 12.2) | − | + | + | − |
| 4 | (20.5, 8.8) | − | + | + | − |
| 5 | (21.6, 8.8) | − | − | − | − |
| 6 | (21.5, 9.4) | − | − | − | − |
| 7 | (21.4, 11.4) | − | + | + | − |

**Artifact 186.** This tool was examined at 7 locations, and fat and resin residues were noted at all but two loci (5 and 6), which is probably the region of a fracture. The least that can be stated is that the tool was used on animal tissue as fat residue would indicate. The resin may either have resulted from use on wood or from hafting. Fat residue in the absence of blood may indicate that the tool was used on cooked flesh.

*Appendix 4*

**ARTIFACT RESIDUE ANALYSIS FORM**     Artifact # __189__

Sample Locations

0 ———— 3 CM

**Results:**

| Locus | Grid Location (x,y) | Blood | Fat | Resin | Starch |
|-------|---------------------|-------|-----|-------|--------|
| 1 | (14.4, 11.5) | + | + | − | + |
| 2 | (20.3, 11.2) | − | + | − | + |

**Artifact 189.** This tool was examined at 2 locations. Blood, fat, and starch residues were recovered from one locus, and fat and starch from the other. Differentiation of residues was insufficient to allow the determination of how the tool was used, although it can be stated that the tool was used on both plant and animal tissue.

**ARTIFACT RESIDUE ANALYSIS FORM**  Artifact # 198
Sample Locations

0    3 CM

Results:

| Locus | Grid Location (x,y) | Blood | Fat | Resin | Starch |
|---|---|---|---|---|---|
| 1 | (14.8, 11.1) | – | – | – | – |
| 2 | (14.9, 12.2) | – | – | – | – |
| 3 | (20.1, 10.8) | – | – | – | – |
| 4 | (20.4, 13.2) | – | – | – | – |

**Artifact 198.** This artifact was examined at 4 locations, and no residues were found.

*Appendix 4*  125

## ARTIFACT RESIDUE ANALYSIS FORM     Artifact # __199__
Sample Locations

0        3 CM

Results:

| Locus | Grid Location (x,y) | Blood | Fat | Resin | Starch |
|---|---|---|---|---|---|
| 1 | (13.0, 11.0) | – | – | + | – |
| 2 | (12.5, 11.4) | – | – | – | – |
| 3 | (13.4, 11.7) | – | – | – | – |
| 4 | (12.4, 14.4) | – | + | – | – |
| 5 | (17.7, 11.4) | – | – | + | – |
| 6 | (18.0, 14.9) | – | + | – | – |

**Artifact 199.** This tool was examined at 6 locations. Resin was found at the narrower protrusion (loci 1 and 5). Fat was found on the broader region (loci 4 and 6). The resin may have resulted from pitch being used as a fixative in hafting, and the presence of fat indicates that the artifact was used on animal tissue. The presence of fat without blood residue may indicate that the tool was used on cooked flesh.

**ARTIFACT RESIDUE ANALYSIS FORM**     Artifact # __204__

Sample Locations

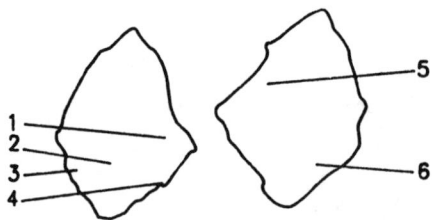

0           3 CM

**Results:**

| Locus | Grid Location (x,y) | Blood | Fat | Resin | Starch |
|---|---|---|---|---|---|
| 1 | (11.6, 11.0) | — | — | — | — |
| 2 | (9.4, 12.1) | — | — | — | — |
| 3 | (8.0, 12.3) | — | — | — | — |
| 4 | (11.4, 12.8) | — | — | — | — |
| 5 | (16.0, 9.9) | — | — | — | — |
| 6 | (18.0, 12.2) | — | — | — | — |

**Artifact 204.** Six loci were examined on this tool and no residues were found.

*Appendix 4*    127

## ARTIFACT RESIDUE ANALYSIS FORM

Artifact # 208

**Sample Locations**

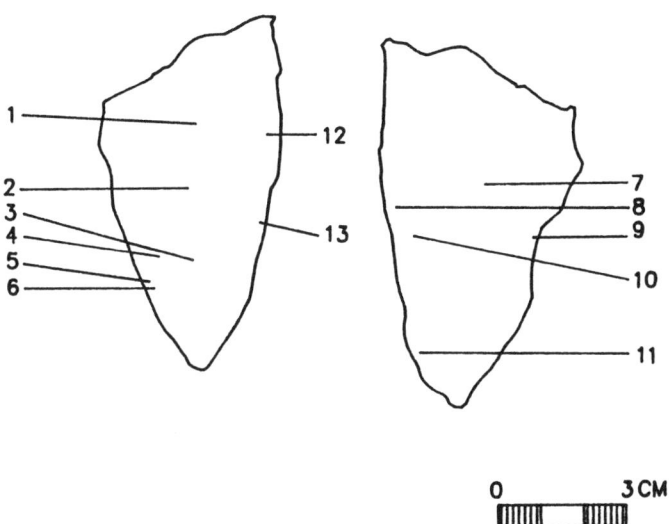

**Results:**

| Locus | Grid Location (x,y) | Blood | Fat | Resin | Starch |
|---|---|---|---|---|---|
| 1 | (11.0, 6.9) | − | + | − | − |
| 2 | (10.6, 9.6) | − | + | − | − |
| 3 | (10.8, 12.3) | − | + | − | − |
| 4 | (9.4, 12.2) | + | + | − | − |
| 5 | (9.0, 13.2) | − | + | + | − |
| 6 | (9.2, 13.6) | + | + | + | − |
| 7 | (23.2, 9.5) | − | + | − | − |
| 8 | (19.3, 10.4) | − | + | − | − |
| 9 | (25.0, 11.6) | + | + | − | − |
| 10 | (20.1, 11.5) | − | + | − | − |
| 11 | (20.4, 16.4) | − | + | − | − |
| 12 | (14.0, 7.4) | − | + | − | − |
| 13 | (13.6, 11.0) | − | + | − | − |

**Artifact 208.** This tool was examined at 13 loci. Blood, fat, and resin residues were identified at various locations on both sides. Both sides of one edge (loci 8, 11, 12, and 13) have only fat residue in the absence of blood. Fat is also exclusively present on the central region of the tool (loci 1, 2, 3, and 7). This might suggest that the opposite edge was the one used most frequently (loci 4, 5, 6, and 9). The tool was likely used as a knife on both wood and animal tissue.

*128*  *Foxie Otter Site*

**ARTIFACT RESIDUE ANALYSIS FORM**  Artifact # __345__
Sample Locations

0         3 CM

**Results:**

| Locus | Grid Location (x,y) | Blood | Fat | Resin | Starch |
|---|---|---|---|---|---|
| 1 | (16.9, 9.2) | – | – | – | – |
| 2 | (22.0, 8.9) | – | – | – | – |

**Artifact 345.** This artifact was examined at 2 locations and no residues were identified.

*Appendix 4*

**ARTIFACT RESIDUE ANALYSIS FORM**   Artifact # __355__

**Sample Locations**

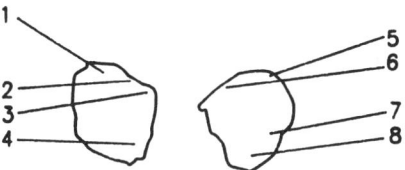

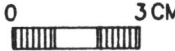

0          3 CM

**Results:**

| Locus | Grid Location (x,y) | Blood | Fat | Resin | Starch |
|-------|---------------------|-------|-----|-------|--------|
| 1 | (13.3, 11.3) | − | − | + | − |
| 2 | (14.5, 12.3) | − | − | + | − |
| 3 | (15.2, 12.6) | − | − | + | − |
| 4 | (14.5, 14.7) | − | − | − | − |
| 5 | (20.3, 11.9) | − | − | + | − |
| 6 | (18.4, 12.4) | − | − | + | − |
| 7 | (20.4, 14.3) | − | − | − | + |
| 8 | (19.5, 15.4) | − | − | − | + |

**Artifact 355.** This tool was examined at 8 loci, and resin residue was found along the thick edge (loci 1, 2, 3, 5, and 6) and starch was identified along the opposite edge (loci 7 and 8). It is possible that the resin is indicative of hafting. The opposing edge was evidently used to process plant matter as starch is present.

**ARTIFACT RESIDUE ANALYSIS FORM**   Artifact # __393__
Sample Locations

0     3 CM

**Results:**

| Locus | Grid Location (x,y) | Blood | Fat | Resin | Starch |
|-------|---------------------|-------|-----|-------|--------|
| 1     | (16.9, 9.2)         | –     | –   | –     | –      |
| 2     | (22.0, 8.9)         | –     | –   | –     | –      |

**Artifact 393.** This artifact was examined at 2 locations and no residues were found.

*Appendix 4*

**ARTIFACT RESIDUE ANALYSIS FORM**　　　　　　　Artifact # __396__

**Sample Locations**

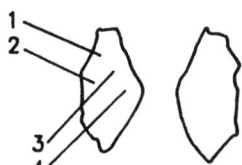

0　　　3 CM

**Results:**

| Locus | Grid Location (x,y) | Blood | Fat | Resin | Starch |
|---|---|---|---|---|---|
| 1 | (12.8, 10.8) | − | + | + | − |
| 2 | (12.5, 11.9) | − | + | − | − |
| 3 | (13.4, 11.5) | − | + | + | − |
| 4 | (14.0, 12.2) | − | + | − | − |

**Artifact 396.** This tool was examined at 4 locations. Fat and resin residues were identified. The presence of resin may either indicate that the tool was used for wood-working or that resin in the form of pitch was used as a fixative for hafting purposes. Fat residue indicates that the tool was used on animal tissue, and fat in the absence of blood residue may indicate that the tool was used on cooked flesh.

**ARTIFACT RESIDUE ANALYSIS FORM**         Artifact #  __419___
Sample Locations

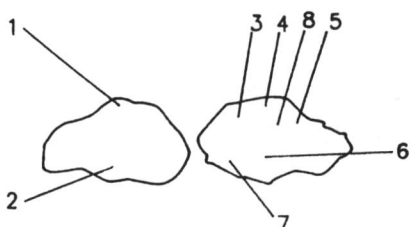

0      3 CM

**Results:**

| Locus | Grid Location (x,y) | Blood | Fat | Resin | Starch |
|---|---|---|---|---|---|
| 1 | (13.5, 10.5) | + | + | − | − |
| 2 | (13.3, 13.2) | − | − | − | − |
| 3 | (18.6, 11.1) | + | + | − | − |
| 4 | (19.6, 10.6) | + | + | − | − |
| 5 | (21.1, 11.2) | + | + | − | − |
| 6 | (19.7, 12.7) | − | − | − | − |
| 7 | (18.2, 12.8) | − | − | − | − |
| 8 | (20.3, 11.3) | + | + | − | − |

**Artifact 419.** This tool was examined at 8 loci and only blood and fat residues were identified, and 3 loci (2, 6, and 7) were barren of residues. This barren region may indicate some form of hafting without the use of resin as a fixative. As all of the residues tend to occur near the steep edge of the tool, it may have been used as a scraper.

*Appendix 4*

**ARTIFACT RESIDUE ANALYSIS FORM**              Artifact # __420___

Sample Locations

0          3 CM

**Results:**

| Locus | Grid Location (x,y) | Blood | Fat | Resin | Starch |
|-------|---------------------|-------|-----|-------|--------|
| 1     | (28.8, 7.3)         | —     | —   | —     | —      |
| 2     | (20.5, 9.3)         | —     | —   | —     | —      |

**Artifact 420.** This tool was examined at 2 locations and no residues were found.

**ARTIFACT RESIDUE ANALYSIS FORM**               Artifact # __423__

Sample Locations

0　　　　3 CM

**Results:**

| Locus | Grid Location (x,y) | Blood | Fat | Resin | Starch |
|---|---|---|---|---|---|
| 1 | (13.7, 10.4) | – | + | – | – |
| 2 | (13.8, 10.9) | – | + | – | – |
| 3 | (16.9, 10.5) | – | + | – | – |
| 4 | (16.6, 11.2) | – | + | – | – |

**Artifact 423.** This tool was examined at 4 locations and fat residue was found at each. The tool, therefore, was used on animal tissue, and the presence of fat residue in the absence of blood may indicate that the tool was used on cooked flesh.

*Appendix 4* 135

## ARTIFACT RESIDUE ANALYSIS FORM

Artifact # __463__

Sample Locations

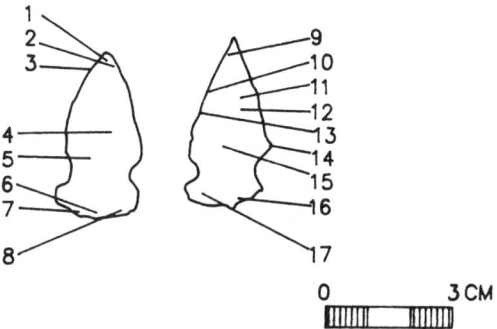

Results:

| Locus | Grid Location (x,y) | Blood | Fat | Resin | Starch |
|---|---|---|---|---|---|
| 1 | (14.4, 8.4) | – | – | – | – |
| 2 | (14.5, 8.6) | – | – | – | – |
| 3 | (13.6, 8.8) | – | – | – | – |
| 4 | (14.5, 11.4) | – | – | – | – |
| 5 | (13.6, 12.4) | – | – | – | – |
| 6 | (14.0, 14.6) | – | – | + | – |
| 7 | (13.2, 14.5) | – | – | + | – |
| 8 | (15.0, 14.4) | – | – | + | – |
| 9 | (19.5, 8.3) | – | – | – | – |
| 10 | (8.6, 9.7) | – | – | – | – |
| 11 | (20.0, 10.0) | – | – | – | – |
| 12 | (20.0, 10.5) | – | – | – | – |
| 13 | (18.5, 10.6) | – | – | – | – |
| 14 | (21.2, 11.9) | – | – | – | – |
| 15 | (19.3, 11.9) | – | – | – | – |
| 16 | (19.8, 13.8) | – | – | + | – |
| 17 | (18.5, 14.1) | – | – | + | – |

**Artifact 463.** This tool was examined at 17 loci. Resin was the only residue found. It was recovered from loci 6, 7, 8, 11, and 17. This is the type of situation that one would expect in the case of a tool used as a projectile point. Here, resin would likely be used as a fixative in halfting. The lack of other residues could result from either the tool having never hit its mark, or the time of penetration of the tool in an animal was too brief to allow an accumulation of residue.

**ARTIFACT RESIDUE ANALYSIS FORM**                    Artifact # __464__

Sample Locations

 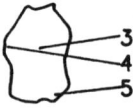

0      3 CM

**Results:**

| Locus | Grid Location (x,y) | Blood | Fat | Resin | Starch |
|---|---|---|---|---|---|
| 1 | (14.5, 9.0)  | + | + | − | − |
| 2 | (15.0, 11.4) | − | − | + | − |
| 3 | (21.5, 8.9)  | + | + | − | − |
| 4 | (20.2, 8.8)  | + | + | − | − |
| 5 | (22.2, 10.7) | − | − | + | − |

**Artifact 464.** This tool was examined at 5 locations. Blood and fat were found at loci 1, 3 and 4; resin was identified at 2 and 5 on the base. While the resin likely indicates hafting, blood and fat may indicate that the tool was a projectile point which hit its mark, or that the tool was used for cutting and scraping animal tissue. The tool may also be a broken and reused projectile point.

*Appendix 4*  137

**ARTIFACT RESIDUE ANALYSIS FORM**    Artifact # __477___

**Sample Locations**

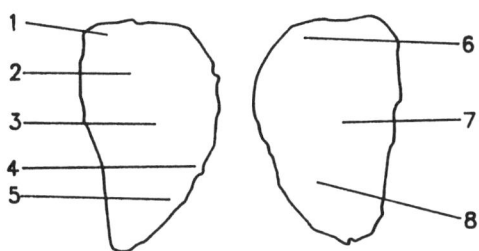

0    3 CM

**Results:**

| Locus | Grid Location (x,y) | Blood | Fat | Resin | Starch |
|---|---|---|---|---|---|
| 1 | (10.0, 8.0) | – | – | + | – |
| 2 | (11.3, 9.7) | – | – | + | – |
| 3 | (12.4, 11.7) | – | + | – | – |
| 4 | (14.0, 13.4) | – | + | – | – |
| 5 | (13.0, 14.6) | – | + | – | – |
| 6 | (18.5, 8.3) | – | + | – | – |
| 7 | (20.0, 11.8) | – | + | – | – |
| 8 | (19.1, 14.0) | – | + | – | – |

**Artifact 477.** This tool was examined at 8 loci. Fat residue was found at all but loci 1 and 2 which contained resin. The resin likely indicates hafting, while the fat residue indicates use on animal tissue. As fat is present without blood, there is a possibility that the tool was used on cooked flesh.

## ARTIFACT RESIDUE ANALYSIS FORM
Sample Locations

Artifact # __4220__

0　　　3 CM

**Results:**

| Locus | Grid Location (x,y) | Blood | Fat | Resin | Starch |
|---|---|---|---|---|---|
| 1 | (11.7, 10.9) | – | – | – | – |
| 2 | (12.8, 11.0) | – | – | – | – |
| 3 | (16.6, 9.9) | – | – | – | – |
| 4 | (18.1, 11.5) | – | – | – | – |

**Artifact 4220.** This artifact was examined at 4 loci, and no residues were recovered.

*Appendix 4*

**ARTIFACT RESIDUE ANALYSIS FORM**  Artifact # __4221__

**Sample Locations**

0　　　3 CM

**Results:**

| Locus | Grid Location (x,y) | Blood | Fat | Resin | Starch |
|---|---|---|---|---|---|
| 1 | (15.0, 10.1) | – | – | – | – |
| 2 | (19.0, 10.0) | – | – | – | – |

**Artifact 4221.** This artifact was examined at 2 loci and no residues were recovered.

*Foxie Otter Site*

**ARTIFACT RESIDUE ANALYSIS FORM**           Artifact # 4253

Sample Locations

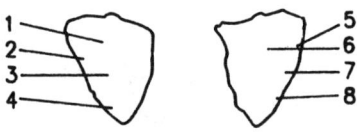

**Results:**

| Locus | Grid Location (x,y) | Blood | Fat | Resin | Starch |
|---|---|---|---|---|---|
| 1 | (15.1, 8.3) | + | + | − | − |
| 2 | (14.4, 9.0) | − | − | − | − |
| 3 | (15.4, 9.6) | + | + | − | − |
| 4 | (15.5, 11.0) | − | − | − | − |
| 5 | (23.3, 8.3) | − | − | − | − |
| 6 | (22.0, 8.6) | + | + | − | − |
| 7 | (22.6, 9.5) | + | + | − | − |
| 8 | (22.4, 10.5) | − | − | − | − |

**Artifact 4253.** This tool was examined at 8 loci, and blood and fat residues were located away from the edge of the tool. The implement was apparently used on animal tissue.

*Appendix 4*

**ARTIFACT RESIDUE ANALYSIS FORM**

Sample Locations

Artifact # __4271__

Results:

| Locus | Grid Location (x,y) | Blood | Fat | Resin | Starch |
|---|---|---|---|---|---|
| 1 | (11.8, 9.5) | – | – | – | – |
| 2 | (12.5, 10.1) | – | – | – | – |
| 3 | (13.0, 10.3) | – | – | – | – |
| 4 | (21.0, 8.4) | – | – | + | – |
| 5 | (20.6, 10.6) | – | – | + | – |
| 6 | (19.0, 11.6) | – | – | + | – |

**Artifact 4271.** This tool was examined at 6 locations, and resin was identified at loci 4, 5, and 6. The tool may be a broken biface stem where resin would have been used as an aid to hafting.

## ARTIFACT RESIDUE ANALYSIS FORM

Artifact # 4272

Sample Locations

0      3 CM

**Results:**

| Locus | Grid Location (x,y) | Blood | Fat | Resin | Starch |
|---|---|---|---|---|---|
| 1 | (15.0, 10.4) | – | – | – | – |
| 2 | (14.6, 11.9) | – | – | – | – |
| 3 | (19.8, 9.8) | – | – | – | – |
| 4 | (20.7, 10.1) | – | – | – | – |

**Artifact 4272.** This artifact was examined at 4 loci and no residues were found.

*Appendix 4*    143

**ARTIFACT RESIDUE ANALYSIS FORM**    Artifact # __4278__

Sample Locations

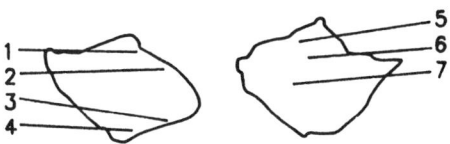

0    3 CM

Results:

| Locus | Grid Location (x,y) | Blood | Fat | Resin | Starch |
|---|---|---|---|---|---|
| 1 | (11.6, 9.6) | − | + | − | − |
| 2 | (12.7, 10.4) | − | + | − | − |
| 3 | (12.8, 12.4) | − | + | − | − |
| 4 | (11.4, 12.8) | − | + | − | − |
| 5 | (18.4, 8.4) | − | + | − | − |
| 6 | (18.8, 9.1) | − | + | − | − |
| 7 | (18.3, 12.0) | − | − | − | − |

**Artifact 4278.** The presence of fat residue at 6 of the 7 locations tested indicates that the tool was used on animal tissue. Fat residue in the absence of blood residue may indicate that the tool was used on cooked flesh.

## ARTIFACT RESIDUE ANALYSIS FORM

Artifact # 4279

Sample Locations

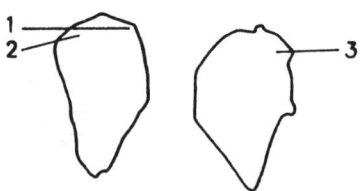

0          3 CM

**Results:**

| Locus | Grid Location (x,y) | Blood | Fat | Resin | Starch |
|-------|---------------------|-------|-----|-------|--------|
| 1 | (18.0, 6.6) | + | + | − | − |
| 2 | (16.0, 7.0) | + | + | − | − |
| 3 | (24.2, 7.5) | − | − | − | − |

**Artifact 4279.** The presence of blood and fat residues on 2 of the 3 loci tested indicates that this tool was used on animal tissue.

*Appendix 4*    *145*

**ARTIFACT RESIDUE ANALYSIS FORM**        Artifact # __4289__

Sample Locations

Results:

| Locus | Grid Location (x,y) | Blood | Fat | Resin | Starch |
|---|---|---|---|---|---|
| 1 | (18.1, 9.9) | — | — | — | — |
| 2 | (21.2, 10.1) | — | — | — | — |

**Artifact 4289.** This artifact was examined at 2 loci and no residues were found.

## ARTIFACT RESIDUE ANALYSIS FORM

Artifact # 4309

Sample Locations

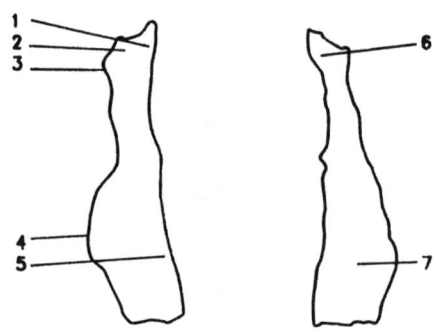

Results:

| Locus | Grid Location (x,y) | Blood | Fat | Resin | Starch |
|-------|---------------------|-------|-----|-------|--------|
| 1 | (13.5, 5.5) | -- | -- | -- | -- |
| 2 | (12.6, 5.7) | -- | -- | -- | -- |
| 3 | (11.8, 6.4) | -- | -- | -- | -- |
| 4 | (11.3, 13.3) | -- | -- | -- | -- |
| 5 | (14.4, 14.2) | -- | -- | -- | -- |
| 6 | (20.8, 6.0) | -- | -- | -- | -- |
| 7 | (22.4, 14.4) | -- | -- | -- | -- |

**Artifact 4309.** This artifact was examined at 7 loci and no residues were found.

## Summary and Conclusions

A total of 40 tools from the Foxie Otter site were examined for blood, fat, resin, and starch residues in this study using chemical spot tests. Of the artifacts tested, 27 contained various combinations of these residues, and 13 were barren of residues.

The following 13 artifacts contained no residue deposits at any of the loci examined: 78, 83, 162, 198, 204, 345, 393, 420, 4220, 4221, 4272, 4289, and 4309. The possible reasons for this lack of residues are numerous. It is possible that they were never used as tools, but were deposited at the site as waste flakes or shatter during tool manufacture. It is also possible that they were used on inorganic matter such as stone, and thus no residue would be expected. Perhaps these tools were exposed to heat, either natural heat occurring in a forest fire, or heated in a hearth accidentally or purpose to treat the material. Finally, there is a possibility that chemical and biotic microenvironments contacting these artifacts in the soil may not have been conducive to the longevity of residues of these tools compared to the tools which had residues.

Artifacts which exhibited residues are listed against categories describing the different combinations of residues found in Table 4.1. Eleven such categories are listed, including: fat; fat and blood; fat, blood, and starch; resin; resin where hafting is suspected; resin and fat; resin and fat where hafting is suspected; resin, blood and fat; resin, blood and fat where hafting is suspected; resin and starch where hafting is suspected; and all residues. Artifacts are listed against these categories by number.

From Table 4.1, it is readily apparent that the largest category of residues is "blood and fat." It is interesting to note from the results that artifacts 134 and 419 in this category were suspected of being scrapers, as were 163 and 464 in the "resin, blood and fat (hafted)" category. The rest of these are either general cutting implements or fragments of larger cutting tools. It is reasonable to assume, therefore, that a certain amount of butchering and perhaps hide processing occurred at the Foxie Otter site.

It is useful to group these artifacts into the following broader categories based on the residues present on them: tools that were used on animal tissue; tools that were used on plant tissue; and tools that were used on both plant and animal tissue. A further category may be formed to include those tools that were apparently used on cooked flesh. This category is derived from the presence of fat residue in the absence of blood residue. It includes artifacts used on animals, and those used on both plants and animals. Table 4.2 below lists the artifacts with respect to these categories. Artifacts 463 and 4271 are excluded from this as they show only residues demonstrating hafting.

Again from Table 4.2, the largest category is animal use, where 16 of the

TABLE 4.1
Listing Artifacts by Number Against Residue Categories

| Residue Category | Artifacts |
| --- | --- |
| Fat | 423, 4278 |
| Fat and blood | 134, 149, 156, 184, 419, 4279, 4253 |
| Fat, blood, and starch | 180, 189 |
| Resin | 164, 171, 172 |
| Resin (hafted) | 463, 4271 |
| Resin and fat | 186, 477 |
| Resin and fat (hafted) | 199, 396 |
| Resin, blood and fat | 173, 208 |
| Resin, blood and fat (hafted) | 75, 163, 464 |
| Resin, and starch (hafted) | 355 |
| All residues | 34 |

TABLE 4.2
Classification of Tools According to their Use

| Animal | Plant | Plant and Animal | Cooked Flesh |
| --- | --- | --- | --- |
| 78 | 164 | 34 | 186 |
| 134 | 171 | 173 | 199 |
| 149 | 172 | 180 | 396 |
| 156 | 355 | 189 | 423 |
| 163 | | 208 | 477 |
| 184 | | | 4278 |
| 186 | | | |
| 199 | | | |
| 396 | | | |
| 419 | | | |
| 423 | | | |
| 464 | | | |
| 477 | | | |
| 4253 | | | |
| 4278 | | | |
| 4279 | | | |

27 artifacts with residue were apparently used on animal tissue. Six of these 16 appear to have been used on cooked flesh, and 5 artifacts were evidently used on both plant and animal tissue. Four artifacts were used on plant material, and 3 of these were used on wood.

It is tempting to construct a small scenario of the type of activities which may have been carried out at the site using this information. First, the large number of artifacts that are barren of residue probably indicates that a certain amount of tool making was carried out at the site. It would be interesting to know if there was a quarry nearby, and what percentage of the total lithic assemblage these 13 barren tools represent. Second, as the largest number of tools with residues were evidently used on animal tissue, it is reasonable to conclude that a fair amount of butchering took place there. Furthermore, as some of these tools may be identified as scrapers, this butchering might be related to hide processing. Some of the artifacts displaying residues were likely used on cooked flesh. This would indicate that some food preparation and consumption was carried out. Finally, it is evident that some woodworking was carried out as three of the four tools used on plant material were apparently used on wood. In conclusion, this study indicates that at least four types of activities were carried out at the Foxie Otter site. These activities may be ranked as follows: tool making, butchering and most likely hide processing, food preparation and consumption, and wood-working.

## PART 2. Residue Analysis of Selected Debitage

This section reports the residue analysis results of 45 flakes recovered from the Foxie Otter site. Whereas the previous section examined worked tools for traces of residue, this part examines flakage. The results of both studies will be combined with the provenance information on tools to attempt to generate a hypothesis concerning site use. The methods used to sample and analyze residues are discussed at the beginning of this appendix.

**ARTIFACT RESIDUE ANALYSIS FORM**  Artifact # __435__
Sample Locations

0         3 CM

Results:

| Locus | Grid Location (x,y) | Blood | Fat | Resin | Starch |
|-------|---------------------|-------|-----|-------|--------|
| 1     | –                   | –     | –   | –     | –      |
| 2     | –                   | –     | –   | –     | –      |

**Artifact 435.** This artifact was examined at 2 loci and no residues were recovered.

*Appendix 4*  151

## ARTIFACT RESIDUE ANALYSIS FORM

Artifact # __436__

Sample Locations

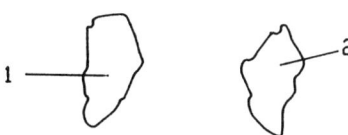

0    3 CM

Results:

| Locus | Grid Location (x,y) | Blood | Fat | Resin | Starch |
|---|---|---|---|---|---|
| 1 | -- | -- | -- | -- | -- |
| 2 | -- | -- | -- | -- | -- |

**Artifact 436.** This artifact was examined at 2 loci and no residues were recovered.

**ARTIFACT RESIDUE ANALYSIS FORM**  Artifact # __448__

Sample Locations

0      3 CM

Results:

| Locus | Grid Location (x,y) | Blood | Fat | Resin | Starch |
|-------|---------------------|-------|-----|-------|--------|
| 1 | – | – | – | – | – |
| 2 | – | – | – | – | – |

**Artifact 448.** This artifact was examined at 2 loci and no residues were recovered.

*Appendix 4* 153

ARTIFACT RESIDUE ANALYSIS FORM         Artifact # __449__
Sample Locations

0         3 CM

Results:

| Locus | Grid Location (x,y) | Blood | Fat | Resin | Starch |
|-------|---------------------|-------|-----|-------|--------|
| 1     | –                   | –     | –   | –     | –      |
| 2     | –                   | –     | –   | –     | –      |

**Artifact 449.** This artifact was examined at 2 locations, and no residues were recovered.

*154*     *Foxie Otter Site*

**ARTIFACT RESIDUE ANALYSIS FORM**     Artifact # __450__

Sample Locations

0     3 CM

Results:

| Locus | Grid Location (x,y) | Blood | Fat | Resin | Starch |
|---|---|---|---|---|---|
| 1 | – | – | – | – | – |
| 2 | – | – | – | – | – |

**Artifact 450.** This artifact was examined at 2 loci and no residues were recovered.

*Appendix 4*          *155*

## ARTIFACT RESIDUE ANALYSIS FORM                 Artifact # __465___
Sample Locations

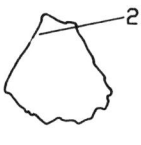

0       3 CM

Results:

| Locus | Grid Location (x,y) | Blood | Fat | Resin | Starch |
|-------|---------------------|-------|-----|-------|--------|
| 1     | –                   | –     | –   | –     | –      |
| 2     | –                   | –     | –   | –     | –      |

**Artifact 465.** This flake was examined at 2 loci and no residues were recovered.

*156*  *Foxie Otter Site*

**ARTIFACT RESIDUE ANALYSIS FORM**  Artifact # __466__

Sample Locations

 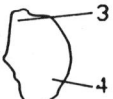

0        3 CM

Results:

| Locus | Grid Location (x,y) | Blood | Fat | Resin | Starch |
|-------|---------------------|-------|-----|-------|--------|
| 1 | – | – | – | – | – |
| 2 | – | – | – | – | – |
| 3 | – | – | – | – | – |
| 4 | – | – | – | – | – |

**Artifact 466.** This flake was examined at 4 loci, and no residues were recovered.

*Appendix 4*

**ARTIFACT RESIDUE ANALYSIS FORM**  Artifact # __468___

Sample Locations

 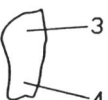

0    3 CM

Results:

| Locus | Grid Location (x,y) | Blood | Fat | Resin | Starch |
|-------|---------------------|-------|-----|-------|--------|
| 1 | – | + | + | – | – |
| 2 | – | + | + | – | – |
| 3 | – | – | – | – | – |
| 4 | – | – | – | – | – |

**Artifact 468.** This artifact was examined at 4 loci, and blood and fat residues were recovered from loci 1 and 2 on one surface. The absence of residue on one surface may indicate that the tool is a fragment, and possibly a resharpening or reforming flake from a tool used to process animal tissue.

## ARTIFACT RESIDUE ANALYSIS FORM

Artifact # 470

Sample Locations

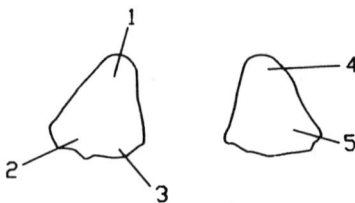

0   3 CM

Results:

| Locus | Grid Location (x,y) | Blood | Fat | Resin | Starch |
|---|---|---|---|---|---|
| 1 | – | –– | + | – | – |
| 2 | – | – | + | – | – |
| 3 | – | – | + | – | – |
| 4 | – | – | + | – | – |
| 5 | – | – | + | – | – |

**Artifact 470.** This flake was examined at 5 loci, and fat residue was found at each. The tool was apparently used on animal tissue, and fat residue in the absence of blood might indicate that the tool was used to process cooked flesh.

*Appendix 4* 

## ARTIFACT RESIDUE ANALYSIS FORM    Artifact # _472___

Sample Locations

Results:

| Locus | Grid Location (x,y) | Blood | Fat | Resin | Starch |
|-------|---------------------|-------|-----|-------|--------|
| 1 | – | – | – | – | – |
| 2 | – | – | – | – | – |

**Artifact 472.** This flake was examined at 2 loci and no residues were recovered.

**ARTIFACT RESIDUE ANALYSIS FORM**                Artifact #  478

Sample Locations

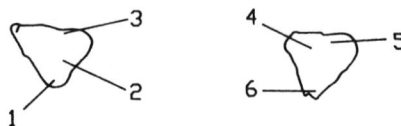

Results:

| Locus | Grid Location (x,y) | Blood | Fat | Resin | Starch |
|---|---|---|---|---|---|
| 1 | − | − | − | + | − |
| 2 | − | − | + | − | − |
| 3 | − | − | + | − | − |
| 4 | − | − | + | − | − |
| 5 | − | − | + | − | − |
| 6 | − | − | − | + | − |

**Artifact 478.** This flake was examined at 6 loci and fat was found across the broad thin region, while resin was recovered from the comparatively stout apex. It is suggested that the tool was hafted at the robust apex with resin used as a fixative. Fat residue, in the absence of blood, may indicate that the tool was used on cooked flesh.

*Appendix 4*

ARTIFACT RESIDUE ANALYSIS FORM          Artifact # __481___

Sample Locations

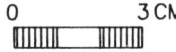

Results:

| Locus | Grid Location (x,y) | Blood | Fat | Resin | Starch |
|-------|---------------------|-------|-----|-------|--------|
| 1     | –                   | –     | +   | –     | –      |
| 2     | –                   | –     | +   | –     | –      |
| 3     | –                   | –     | –   | –     | –      |

**Artifact 481.** This artifact was examined at 3 loci, and fat residue was found on only one surface. Thus, for the same reason as artifact 468, this artifact might be a resharpening flake. Fat in the absence of blood might indicate that the tool was used on cooked tissue.

## ARTIFACT RESIDUE ANALYSIS FORM

Artifact # __482___

Sample Locations

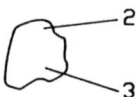

0    3 CM

Results:

| Locus | Grid Location (x,y) | Blood | Fat | Resin | Starch |
|-------|---------------------|-------|-----|-------|--------|
| 1 | – | – | – | – | – |
| 2 | – | – | – | + | – |
| 3 | – | – | – | – | – |

**Artifact 482.** This flake was examined at 3 loci, and only resin residue was recovered from locus 3 on one surface. This may be a tool hafted as artifact 468 above, or it may be a resharpening flake. The absence of resin on the opposite surface would suggest that the latter description is most likely.

*Appendix 4*

## ARTIFACT RESIDUE ANALYSIS FORM

Artifact # _811_

Sample Locations

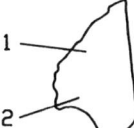 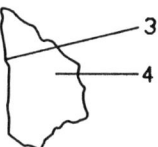

0　　　3 CM

Results:

| Locus | Grid Location (x,y) | Blood | Fat | Resin | Starch |
|---|---|---|---|---|---|
| 1 | – | – | + | – | – |
| 2 | – | – | + | – | – |
| 3 | – | – | + | – | – |
| 4 | – | – | – | – | – |

**Artifact 811.** This artifact was examined at 4 loci, and fat residue was recovered from three. Fat residues were found on the surfaces of the tool, yet no residues were found on the straight edge, suggesting that the tool may have been hafted without the use of resin as a fixative. It may, however, mean that the tool was broken at this point. The tool was apparently used to process animal tissue, and the absence of blood residue may indicate that the tool was used on cooked flesh.

## ARTIFACT RESIDUE ANALYSIS FORM

Artifact # _823__

Sample Locations

0          3 CM

Results:

| Locus | Grid Location (x,y) | Blood | Fat | Resin | Starch |
|---|---|---|---|---|---|
| 1 | – | – | – | – | – |
| 2 | – | – | – | – | – |
| 3 | – | + | + | – | + |
| 4 | – | + | + | – | + |

**Artifact 823.** This tool was examined at 4 loci, and blood, fat and starch residues were found restricted to one surface. The tool, therefore, is likely a flake removed from a larger all purpose tool used to process both plant and animal tissue.

*Appendix 4*   165

ARTIFACT RESIDUE ANALYSIS FORM        Artifact # __824__

Sample Locations

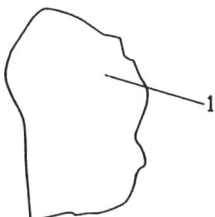
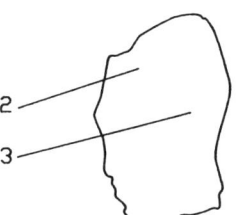

0        3 CM

Results:

| Locus | Grid Location (x,y) | Blood | Fat | Resin | Starch |
|-------|---------------------|-------|-----|-------|--------|
| 1 | – | – | + | – | – |
| 2 | – | – | + | – | – |
| 3 | – | – | + | – | – |

**Artifact 824.** This flake was examined at 3 locations, and was found to contain fat residues at each of the loci tested. The tool was apparently used to process animal tissue, and fat residue in the absence of blood may indicate that the tool was used on cooked flesh.

*166*          *Foxie Otter Site*

**ARTIFACT RESIDUE ANALYSIS FORM**      Artifact # __825__

Sample Locations

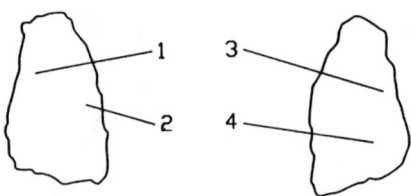

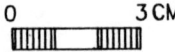

0     3 CM

Results:

| Locus | Grid Location (x,y) | Blood | Fat | Resin | Starch |
|---|---|---|---|---|---|
| 1 | − | + | + | − | − |
| 2 | − | + | + | − | − |
| 3 | − | + | + | − | − |
| 4 | − | + | + | − | − |

**Artifact 825.** This tool was examined at 4 loci, and blood and fat residues were found at each. The tool was apparently used on animal tissue. There is no evidence of hafting in the form of resin residue.

*Appendix 4* 167

## ARTIFACT RESIDUE ANALYSIS FORM        Artifact # __834__

Sample Locations

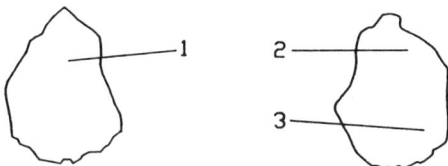

0         3 CM

Results:

| Locus | Grid Location (x,y) | Blood | Fat | Resin | Starch |
|-------|---------------------|-------|-----|-------|--------|
| 1     | –                   | –     | –   | –     | –      |
| 2     | –                   | –     | –   | –     | –      |
| 3     | –                   | –     | –   | –     | –      |

**Artifact 834.** This flake was examined at 3 loci, and no residues were recovered.

**ARTIFACT RESIDUE ANALYSIS FORM**  Artifact # __854__

Sample Locations

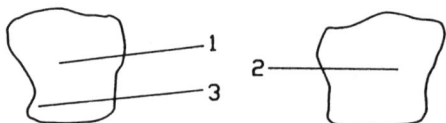

0         3 CM

Results:

| Locus | Grid Location (x,y) | Blood | Fat | Resin | Starch |
|---|---|---|---|---|---|
| 1 | – | – | – | – | – |
| 2 | – | – | – | – | – |
| 3 | – | – | – | – | – |

**Artifact 854.** This flake was examined at 3 loci and no residues were recovered.

*Appendix 4* 169

ARTIFACT RESIDUE ANALYSIS FORM           Artifact # __855___

Sample Locations

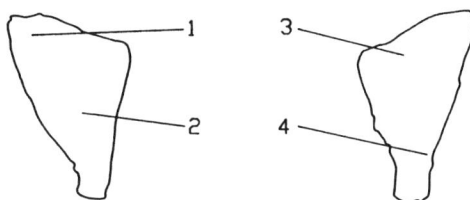

Results:

| Locus | Grid Location (x,y) | Blood | Fat | Resin | Starch |
|-------|---------------------|-------|-----|-------|--------|
| 1 | – | – | + | – | – |
| 2 | – | – | + | – | – |
| 3 | – | – | + | – | – |
| 4 | – | – | + | – | – |

**Artifact 855.** This tool was examined at 4 locations, and fat residue was identified at each. The tool was evidently used to process animal tissue, and likely cooked animal tissue, as fat residue appears in the absence of blood. There was no evidence of hafting in the form of resin residue. The tool was possibly hand-held.

*170*  *Foxie Otter Site*

**ARTIFACT RESIDUE ANALYSIS FORM**  Artifact # _857___

Sample Locations

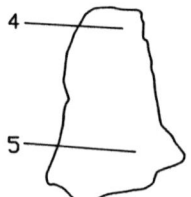

0     3 CM

Results:

| Locus | Grid Location (x,y) | Blood | Fat | Resin | Starch |
|-------|---------------------|-------|-----|-------|--------|
| 1 | - | - | - | - | - |
| 2 | - | - | - | - | - |
| 3 | - | - | - | - | - |
| 4 | - | - | - | - | - |
| 5 | - | - | - | - | - |

**Artifact 857.** This flake was examined at 5 loci and no residues were recovered.

*Appendix 4*

ARTIFACT RESIDUE ANALYSIS FORM              Artifact # _875___

Sample Locations

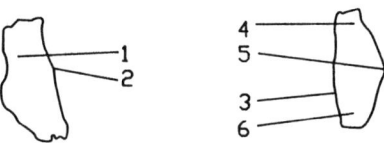

0                3 CM

Results:

| Locus | Grid Location (x,y) | Blood | Fat | Resin | Starch |
|-------|---------------------|-------|-----|-------|--------|
| 1 | − | + | + | + | + |
| 2 | − | − | − | − | − |
| 3 | − | − | − | − | − |
| 4 | − | + | + | + | + |
| 5 | − | − | − | − | − |
| 6 | − | + | + | + | + |

**Artifact 875.** This artifact was examined at 6 loci. Blood, fat, resin and starch residues were found at each loci on the broad area of the tool. Loci 2, 3, and 5 on the edges were barren of residues. This artifact is possibly the middle section of a larger all-purpose tool such as a biface.

*Foxie Otter Site*

**ARTIFACT RESIDUE ANALYSIS FORM**       Artifact # __880__

Sample Locations

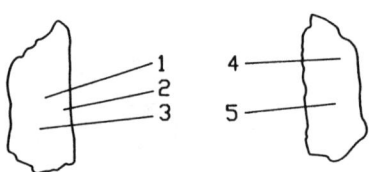

0         3 CM

Results:

| Locus | Grid Location (x,y) | Blood | Fat | Resin | Starch |
|---|---|---|---|---|---|
| 1 | − | + | + | − | − |
| 2 | − | + | + | − | − |
| 3 | − | + | + | − | − |
| 4 | − | − | − | − | − |
| 5 | − | − | − | − | − |

**Artifact 880.** Blood and fat residues were located on one surface of this tool, while the other side was barren. This may indicate that this is a flake removed from a larger tool which was evidently used to process animal tissue.

*Appendix 4* 173

## ARTIFACT RESIDUE ANALYSIS FORM   Artifact # __882__

Sample Locations

 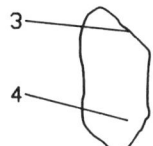

0  3 CM

Results:

| Locus | Grid Location (x,y) | Blood | Fat | Resin | Starch |
|-------|---------------------|-------|-----|-------|--------|
| 1 | – | + | + | – | – |
| 2 | – | + | + | – | – |
| 3 | – | + | + | – | – |
| 4 | – | + | + | – | – |

**Artifact 882.** This tool was examined at 4 loci. Blood and fat residues were recovered from each. The tool, therefore, was apparently used on animal tissue. It contained no resin residues and therefore there is no indication of hafting, hence the tool may have been hand-held.

## ARTIFACT RESIDUE ANALYSIS FORM

Artifact # __883__

Sample Locations

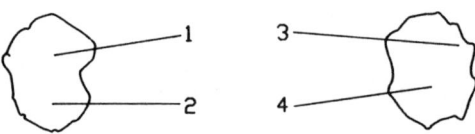

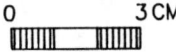

Results:

| Locus | Grid Location (x,y) | Blood | Fat | Resin | Starch |
|-------|---------------------|-------|-----|-------|--------|
| 1 | – | + | + | – | – |
| 2 | – | + | + | – | – |
| 3 | – | – | – | – | – |
| 4 | – | – | – | – | – |

**Artifact 883.** Blood and fat residues on this artifact were restricted to one surface. This likely indicates that it is a resharpening flake from a larger tool used to process animal tissue.

*Appendix 4*                                              175

ARTIFACT RESIDUE ANALYSIS FORM                 Artifact # __4159__

Sample Locations

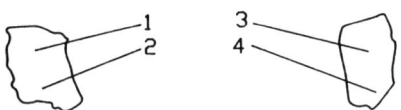

Results:

| Locus | Grid Location (x,y) | Blood | Fat | Resin | Starch |
|-------|---------------------|-------|-----|-------|--------|
| 1 | − | − | − | − | − |
| 2 | − | − | − | − | − |
| 3 | − | − | − | − | − |
| 4 | − | − | − | − | − |

**Artifact 4159.** This artifact was examined at 4 loci and no residues were recovered.

*176*  *Foxie Otter Site*

**ARTIFACT RESIDUE ANALYSIS FORM**         Artifact # __4161__

Sample Locations

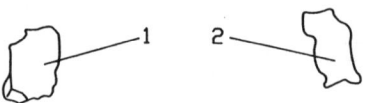

0         3 CM

Results:

| Locus | Grid Location (x,y) | Blood | Fat | Resin | Starch |
|-------|---------------------|-------|-----|-------|--------|
| 1     | –                   | –     | –   | –     | –      |
| 2     | –                   | –     | –   | –     | –      |

**Artifact 4161.** This artifact was examined at 2 loci and no residues were recovered.

*Appendix 4*     *177*

ARTIFACT RESIDUE ANALYSIS FORM               Artifact # __4162__

Sample Locations

Results:

| Locus | Grid Location (x,y) | Blood | Fat | Resin | Starch |
|-------|---------------------|-------|-----|-------|--------|
| 1 | – | – | – | – | – |
| 2 | – | + | + | – | + |
| 3 | – | + | + | – | + |

**Artifact 4162.** This artifact was examined at 3 loci, and blood, fat and starch residues were recovered from the two broad surfaces (loci 1 and 3). The steep narrow edge (loci 1) was barren of residues, indicating that it may have been fractured at this edge rendering it unusable. It is suggested, therefore, that this specimen is a fragment of a larger all-purpose tool used to process both plant and animal tissue.

ARTIFACT RESIDUE ANALYSIS FORM                Artifact # __4203__

Sample Locations

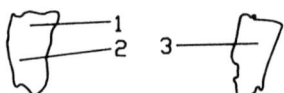

0         3 CM

Results:

| Locus | Grid Location (x,y) | Blood | Fat | Resin | Starch |
|-------|---------------------|-------|-----|-------|--------|
| 1 | − | − | − | − | − |
| 2 | − | − | − | − | − |
| 3 | − | − | − | − | − |

**Artifact 4203.** This artifact was examined at 3 loci and no residues were recovered.

*Appendix 4*

ARTIFACT RESIDUE ANALYSIS FORM     Artifact # __4226__

Sample Locations

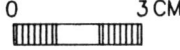

Results:

| Locus | Grid Location (x,y) | Blood | Fat | Resin | Starch |
|-------|---------------------|-------|-----|-------|--------|
| 1 | - | - | - | - | - |
| 2 | - | - | - | - | - |
| 3 | - | - | - | - | - |

**Artifact 4226.** This flake was examined at 3 loci and no residues were recovered.

# ARTIFACT RESIDUE ANALYSIS FORM

Artifact # 4254

Sample Locations

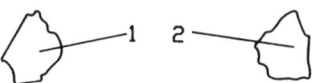

Results:

| Locus | Grid Location (x,y) | Blood | Fat | Resin | Starch |
|-------|---------------------|-------|-----|-------|--------|
| 1 | – | + | + | – | – |
| 2 | – | – | – | – | – |

**Artifact 4254.** This artifact was examined at 2 locations. Blood and fat residues were found on one surface (locus 1). The absence of residue on the other surface indicates that the tool may be a flake off a larger tool used for processing animal tissue.

*Appendix 4*

ARTIFACT RESIDUE ANALYSIS FORM          Artifact # __4255__

Sample Locations

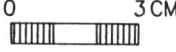

Results:

| Locus | Grid Location (x,y) | Blood | Fat | Resin | Starch |
|-------|---------------------|-------|-----|-------|--------|
| 1 | – | – | – | – | – |
| 2 | – | – | – | – | – |
| 3 | – | – | – | – | – |

**Artifact 4255.** This artifact was examined at 3 locations and no residues were found.

*Foxie Otter Site*

**ARTIFACT RESIDUE ANALYSIS FORM**      Artifact # 4256

Sample Locations

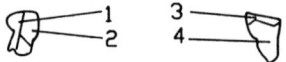

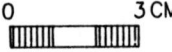

Results:

| Locus | Grid Location (x,y) | Blood | Fat | Resin | Starch |
|---|---|---|---|---|---|
| 1 | − | + | + | − | − |
| 2 | − | − | − | − | − |
| 3 | − | − | − | − | − |
| 4 | − | − | − | − | − |

**Artifact 4256.** This flake was examined at 4 locations. Blood and fat residue were recovered from only one surface (locus 1). All of the other surfaces were barren. It is suggested that this might be consistent with the removal of a flake from a tool used to process animal tissue.

*Appendix 4*                                                                   183

ARTIFACT RESIDUE ANALYSIS FORM                    Artifact # _4257__

Sample Locations

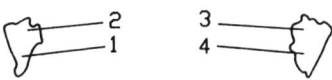

0                3 CM

Results:

| Locus | Grid Location (x,y) | Blood | Fat | Resin | Starch |
|-------|---------------------|-------|-----|-------|--------|
| 1     | –                   | –     | –   | +     | –      |
| 2     | –                   | –     | +   | –     | –      |
| 3     | –                   | –     | +   | –     | –      |
| 4     | –                   | –     | –   | +     | –      |

**Artifact 4257.** The examination of 4 loci revealed the presence of resin in loci 1 and 4 near the apex of the rough triangular shape of the tool. Fat residue was found at loci 2 and 3. This may be a hafted implement used for processing animal tissue, if the resin is considered a fixative. The absence of blood residue may indicate that the tool was used on cooked animal tissue.

*Foxie Otter Site*

ARTIFACT RESIDUE ANALYSIS FORM                Artifact # 4258

Sample Locations

0         3 CM

Results:

| Locus | Grid Location (x,y) | Blood | Fat | Resin | Starch |
|-------|---------------------|-------|-----|-------|--------|
| 1     | –                   | –     | –   | –     | –      |
| 2     | –                   | –     | –   | –     | –      |

**Artifact 4258.** This artifact was examined at 2 loci and no residues were recovered.

*Appendix 4*

ARTIFACT RESIDUE ANALYSIS FORM       Artifact # __4259__

Sample Locations

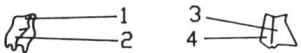

Results:

| Locus | Grid Location (x,y) | Blood | Fat | Resin | Starch |
|-------|---------------------|-------|-----|-------|--------|
| 1 | – | – | – | – | – |
| 2 | – | – | – | – | – |
| 3 | – | + | + | – | – |
| 4 | – | – | – | – | – |

**Artifact 4259.** Four loci were examined on 4259. Both blood and fat residues were found at locus 3. It is suspected that this is a flake that was taken from a larger tool used to process animal tissue.

*Foxie Otter Site*

**ARTIFACT RESIDUE ANALYSIS FORM**  Artifact # 4260

Sample Locations

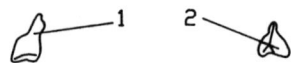

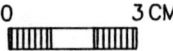

Results:

| Locus | Grid Location (x,y) | Blood | Fat | Resin | Starch |
|-------|---------------------|-------|-----|-------|--------|
| 1 | – | – | – | – | – |
| 2 | – | – | – | – | – |

**Artifact 4260.** This artifact was examined at 2 loci and no residues were recovered.

## ARTIFACT RESIDUE ANALYSIS FORM

Artifact # __4261__

Sample Locations

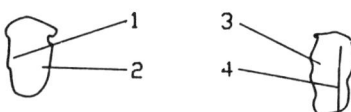

Results:

| Locus | Grid Location (x,y) | Blood | Fat | Resin | Starch |
|-------|---------------------|-------|-----|-------|--------|
| 1 | – | – | + | – | – |
| 2 | – | – | – | + | – |
| 3 | – | – | – | + | – |
| 4 | – | – | + | + | – |

**Artifact 4261.** This flake was examined at 4 loci. Resin residue was identified along one edge (loci 2 and 4) and fat on the opposing side (locus 1) and at the central location (locus 4) with resin. This pattern of residues might indicate that the tool was longitudinally hafted and used as a blade for processing animal tissue. The absence of blood residue likely indicates that the tool was used on cooked flesh.

**ARTIFACT RESIDUE ANALYSIS FORM**  Artifact # __4262__

Sample Locations

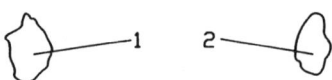

0       3 CM

Results:

| Locus | Grid Location (x,y) | Blood | Fat | Resin | Starch |
|---|---|---|---|---|---|
| 1 | – | – | – | – | – |
| 2 | – | – | – | – | – |

**Artifact 4262.** This artifact was examined in 2 loci and no residues were recovered.

*Appendix 4*

ARTIFACT RESIDUE ANALYSIS FORM        Artifact # __4263__

Sample Locations

Results:

| Locus | Grid Location (x,y) | Blood | Fat | Resin | Starch |
|-------|---------------------|-------|-----|-------|--------|
| 1 | − | − | + | − | − |
| 2 | − | − | − | − | − |

**Artifact 4263.** This artifact was examined at 2 loci. Fat residue was found on one surface. It is likely, therefore, that this is a flake taken from a larger tool, perhaps for resharpening purposes. The larger tool was apparently used on animal tissue. The presence of fat and the absence of blood may indicate its use on cooked flesh.

# ARTIFACT RESIDUE ANALYSIS FORM

Artifact # 4264

Sample Locations

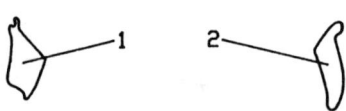

0       3 CM

Results:

| Locus | Grid Location (x,y) | Blood | Fat | Resin | Starch |
|---|---|---|---|---|---|
| 1 | – | – | – | – | – |
| 2 | – | – | – | – | – |

**Artifact 4264.** This artifact was examined in 2 loci and no residues were recovered.

*Appendix 4*

**ARTIFACT RESIDUE ANALYSIS FORM**         Artifact # __4267__

Sample Locations

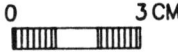

Results:

| Locus | Grid Location (x,y) | Blood | Fat | Resin | Starch |
|-------|---------------------|-------|-----|-------|--------|
| 1 | - | - | - | - | - |
| 2 | - | - | - | - | - |

**Artifact 4267.** This artifact was examined in 2 loci and no residues were recovered.

**ARTIFACT RESIDUE ANALYSIS FORM**          Artifact # __4268__

Sample Locations

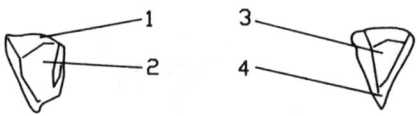

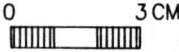

Results:

| Locus | Grid Location (x,y) | Blood | Fat | Resin | Starch |
|-------|--------------------|-------|-----|-------|--------|
| 1 | – | – | – | – | + |
| 2 | – | – | – | – | – |
| 3 | – | – | – | – | – |
| 4 | – | – | – | – | – |

**Artifact 4268.** Starch recovered from locus 1 indicates that this tool was likely used on plant tissue. The lack of residue at other loci probably indicates that the artifact is a resharpening or reshaping flake from a larger tool used for plant processing.

*Appendix 4*            *193*

**ARTIFACT RESIDUE ANALYSIS FORM**            Artifact # __4269__

Sample Locations

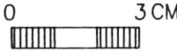

Results:

| Locus | Grid Location (x,y) | Blood | Fat | Resin | Starch |
|-------|---------------------|-------|-----|-------|--------|
| 1     | –                   | –     | –   | –     | –      |
| 2     | –                   | –     | –   | –     | –      |

**Artifact 4269.** This artifact was tested in 2 loci and no residues were recovered.

## ARTIFACT RESIDUE ANALYSIS FORM
Sample Locations

Artifact # __4270__

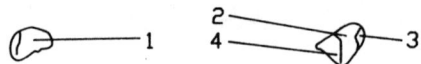

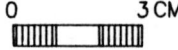
0           3 CM

Results:

| Locus | Grid Location (x,y) | Blood | Fat | Resin | Starch |
|-------|---------------------|-------|-----|-------|--------|
| 1     | -                   | -     | -   | -     | -      |
| 2     | -                   | -     | -   | -     | -      |
| 3     | -                   | -     | -   | -     | -      |
| 4     | -                   | -     | -   | -     | -      |

**Artifact 4270.** This artifact was tested in 4 loci and no residues were recovered.

# PART 3. Results

This section summarizes the results of both the tool and the flakage analysis of Parts 1 and 2 of this appendix. Inferences about function are combined with the provenance data in an attempt to isolate activities being carried out at different locations across the Foxie Otter site.

Site areas A through D were used as the basic geographic unit for this analysis (see Fig. 3 in main text). The results of the residue analysis are presented in tables by site area.

## Area A

Artifacts from area A that were analyzed in this report were recovered from unit E-0 and along the eroding lake bank. Table 4.3 summarizes the data by artifact number, the residues recovered (labeled *B, F, R,* and *S* for blood, fat, resin, and starch), the postulated use, whether or not the artifact was hafted *(H)*, and whether the artifact was a tool fragment *(F)*, for example, a resharpening flake. Notes on the functional interpretation of the tools from the artifact catalog are presented under the heading function. This category reveals assumptions made about individual artifacts by the researchers prior to residue analysis.

Seven of the 115 artifacts (6%) recovered from unit E-0 were examined. Of these, 4 were found to contain residues. Two were evidently used for processing cooked flesh, as fat residues were present in the absence of blood; one was used on raw flesh; and one was apparently used for both plant processing and wood-working. The sample of artifacts examined for residues from this area is too small to make any meaningful speculations about the types of activities that may have been carried out there.

## Area B

Table 4.4 summarizes the artifacts examined for residues in area B. Area B was apparently excavated as a broken transect including units Sc 0N0E to 2N0E inclusively, and 7N0E to 9N0E inclusively. Artifacts selected for this analysis were recovered from units Sc 0N0E, Sc 8N0E, and Sc 1N0E.

Of the 358 flake recovered from area B, 37 were examined for residues. Of these, 15 were barren of residues; 12 were used on animal flesh, 6 of which were likely to have been used on cooked flesh; 6 were used on plant material and with one exception the plant was wood. Two of the tools were

TABLE 4.3
Area A

| Artifact | B F R S[a] | Unit | Concluded Use | H F[b] | Function |
|---|---|---|---|---|---|
| 354 | - - - - | Sc E-0 | — | - - | scraper |
| 355 | - - - - | " | Plant processing, wood work | * - | scraper |
| 393 | - - - - | " | — | - - | scraper |
| 396 | - * * - | " | Animal use, possibly on cooked flesh | * - | — |
| 419 | * * - - | " | Used on animal tissue, possibly as a scraper | * - | — |
| 420 | - - - - | " | — | - - | — |
| 423 | - * - - | Scaler's dock bank | Used on animal possibly used on cooked flesh | - - | — |

[a] B = blood, F = fat, R = resin, S = starch
[b] H = hafted, F = tool fragment

TABLE 4.4
Area B

| Artifact | B F R S[a] | Unit | Concluded Use | H F[b] | Function |
|---|---|---|---|---|---|
| 149 | * * - - | Sc 0N0E | Broken tool or flake from larger tool used on animal tissue | - * | cortex fragment |
| 156 | * * - - | " | Used on animal tissue | - - | flake |
| 162 | - - - - | " | — | - - | flake |
| 163 | * * * - | " | Hafted scraper for use on animal tissue, possibly for hide processing | * - | — |
| 171 | - - * - | " | Use for wood-working obvious as wood fragments are mixed with resin. Likely used as planer or scraper | - - | — |
| 164 | - - * - | " | Possibly used for wood-working, although resin could indicate hafting and disuse | * - | — |
| 172 | - - * - | " | Wood-working | - - | — |
| 173 | * * * - | " | Plant and animal use, likely as knife | ? - | — |
| 180 | * * - * | " | Plant and animal use, likely as knife or chopper | * - | — |

## Appendix 4

| | | | | | |
|---|---|---|---|---|---|
| 184 | * * - - | " | Animal tissue | - - | flake |
| 186 | - * * - | " | Used on wood and animal tissue. Use on cooked flesh suspected | * - | — |
| 189 | * * - * | " | Used on plant and animal tissue | - - | — |
| 198 | - - - - | Sc 0N0E | — | - - | — |
| 199 | - * * - | " | Hafted tool used on animal tissue, and likely on cooked flesh | * - | — |
| 204 | - - - - | " | — | - - | — |
| 208 | * * * - | " | Used on animal tissue, and for wood-working, likely as a knife | - - | — |
| 435 | - - - - | Sc 8N0E | — | - - | — |
| 436 | - - - - | " | — | - - | — |
| 448 | - - - - | " | — | - - | flake |
| 450 | - - - - | " | — | - - | " |
| 463 | - - * - | " | Projectile point | * - | point |
| 464 | * * * - | " | Projectile point that hit its mark, or one that was broken and hafted and used as a knife *or* scraper. Used on animal tissue | | point |
| 465 | - - - - | " | — | - - | flake |
| 466 | - - - - | " | — | - - | flake |
| 468 | * * - - | " | Animal use/ resharpening flake | - * | cortex flake |
| 470 | - * - - | " | Used on cooked animal tissue | - - | — |
| 472 | - - - - | " | — | - - | flake |
| 477 | - * * - | " | Used on cooked animal tissue | * - | scraper |
| 478 | - * * - | " | Used on cooked animal tissue/ resharpening flake | - * | flake |
| 481 | - * - - | " | As above | - * | " |
| 482 | - - * - | " | Resharpening flake | - * | " |
| 4159 | - - - - | Sc 8N0E | — | - - | flake |
| 4161 | - - - - | " | — | - - | " |
| 4162 | * * - * | " | Plant and animal use, resharpening flake | - * | " |
| 4203 | - - - - | " | — | - - | " |

[a]B = blood, F = fat, R = resin, S = starch  
[b]H = hafted, F = tool fragment

used for wood-working, and one of the tools was a projectile point which was barren of all residues but resin, which is taken to be an indication of hafting. Nine of the tools were hafted, and 6 were apparently flakes from larger tools.

## Area C

The results of residue analysis on the one artifact from area C are given in Table 4.5. The tool was apparently a resharpening flake or shatter fragment from a larger tool that was used on both plant and animal tissue. The sample of one tool is insufficient to offer a meaningful statement about the prehistoric use of the area.

## Area D

Table 4.6 below presents the results of residue analysis of artifacts from area D. The artifacts analyzed were from units 38° 0N0E, 38° 14N0W, 38° 0S0E, OS 0S0E, OS 0S0E, and OS 0N0E.

Thirty-seven artifacts from area D were examined for residues. Of these, 17 were barren and 16 were used to process animal tissue, of which 7 were apparently used on cooked animal tissue. One tool was used on non-woody plant material and animal material. One artifact might be the stem fragment of a biface and it is covered in resin which was probably used as a fixative in hafting. Four of the tools examined were deduced to be hafted, and 7 were apparently flakes taken from larger tools.

It will be interesting, perhaps, to compare area B with area D, as these areas exhibited the largest number of artifacts analyzed. To this end, Table 4.7 below presents the attributes from both areas as determined by residue analysis.

Table 4.7 shows the two assemblages similar with two exceptions: area B has only tools that were used for wood-working purposes; and significantly more tools in area B were hafted. Although it is difficult to assess the importance of hafting in assessing the subsistence patterns of the two areas, one can at least conclude that wood-working was carried out in area B and not in area D.

A further analysis of area B shows that many of the tools with blood and fat residues were deduced to be scrapers, both by residue analysis and in the catalog. With this, it might be suggested that area B was a hide processing site. Also, some of the tools show signs of use on cooked flesh, with fat residues but no blood residue present. This might occur as a result of hide processing, as heat is used in hide preparation in some processing methods.

## Appendix 4

TABLE 4.5
Area C

| Artifact | B F R S[a] | Unit | Concluded Use | H F[b] | Function |
|---|---|---|---|---|---|
| 34 | * * * * | B-0 | Resharpening flake or fragment from an all purpose tool. Used on both plant and animal tissue | - * | — |

[a] B = blood, F = fat, R = resin, S = starch
[b] H = hafted, F = tool fragment

TABLE 4.6
Area D

| Artifact | B F R S[a] | Unit | Concluded Use | H F[b] | Function |
|---|---|---|---|---|---|
| 75 | * * * - | 38° 0N0E | Hafted tool used on animal tissue | * - | — |
| 78 | - - - - | " | — | - - | — |
| 83 | - - - - | " | — | - - | — |
| 811 | - * - - | 38° 14N0W | Tool fragment used on animal flesh. Use on cooked flesh suspected | - - | — |
| 823 | * * - * | " | Used on both plant animal tissue. Resharpening flake | | — |
| 825 | * * - - | " | Used on animal tissue | - - | — |
| 824 | - * - - | " | Used on animal tissue, use on cooked flesh suspected | - - | — |
| 834 | - - - - | " | — | - - | — |
| 854 | - - - - | " | — | - - | — |
| 855 | - * - - | " | Used on animal tissue, used on cooked flesh suspected | - - | — |
| 857 | - - - - | " | — | - - | — |
| 875 | * * * * | " | Midsection of an all purpose tool, likely a biface, that was used on both plant and animal tissue | - - | — |
| 880 | * * - - | " | Used on animal tissue, resharpening flake | - * | — |
| 882 | * * - - | " | Used on animal tissue | - - | — |
| 883 | - - - - | 38° 14N0W | — | - - | — |
| 4220 | - - - - | 38° 0S0E | — | - - | — |

| Cat # | B F R S | OS code | Description | H F | Notes |
|---|---|---|---|---|---|
| 4253 | * * - - | OS 0S0E | Used on animal tissue | - - | biface |
| 4256 | * * - - | " | Used on animal tissue, resharpening or reduction flake | - * | — |
| 4257 | - * * - | " | Used on animal tissue, and likely cooked tissue. Tool probably hafted. | * - | — |
| 4258 | - - - - | " | — | - - | — |
| 4259 | * * - - | " | Used on animal tissue, resharpening flake | - * | — |
| 4260 | - - - - | " | — | - - | — |
| 4261 | - * * - | " | Apparently a longitudinally hafted blade used on cooked animal tissue | * - | — |
| 4262 | - - - - | OS 0N0E | — | - - | — |
| 4263 | - * - - | " | Flake from a tool used to process animal tissue. Animal flesh likely cooked | - * | — |
| 4264 | - - - - | " | — | - - | — |
| 4267 | - - - - | " | — | - - | — |
| 4268 | - - - * | " | Used on plant material. Resharpening or reforming or reduction flake from a larger tool | - * | — |
| 4269 | - - - - | " | — | - - | — |
| 4270 | - - - - | " | — | - - | — |
| 4271 | - - * - | OS 0S0E | Apparently the stem portion of a biface fragment | * - | — |
| 4272 | - - - - | OS 0N0E | — | - - | — |
| 4278 | - * - - | " | Used on animal and likely cooked animal flesh | - - | — |
| 4279 | * * - - | " | Used on animal tissue | - - | — |
| 4289 | - - - - | " | — | - - | — |

[a] B = blood, F = fat, R = resin, S = starch
[b] H = hafted, F = tool fragment

TABLE 4.7
Comparison of Attributes of Tools Recovered from Areas B and D

| Attribute | Area B | Area D |
|---|---|---|
| Total examined | 37 | 37 |
| Barren of residues | 15 | 17 |
| Animal use | 12 | 16 |
| Cooked flesh | 6 | 7 |
| Plant use | 2 | 2 |
| Wood-working | 5 | 0 |
| Resharpening flakes | 6 | 7 |
| Hafting | 9 | 4 |

It may be worthwhile to analyze the features of the site to confirm this suspicion.

It is difficult to be as specific in the interpretation of the use of area D. Here, many of the tools were obviously used on animal tissue, but their use was not shown to be in a scraping fashion, and indeed most of the tools were fragments of larger tools or were tools apparently used for cutting flesh. This area may either have been used for general activities, or for rather specific activities such as fish or mammal processing for food purposes. It would be interesting to compare this observation with the other information that was gained in the excavation of the site.

## Conclusion

Most of the tools were found to come from two areas of the site: area B and area D. It is suggested that area B might contain tools that are associated with hide processing, and as a result, it was strongly recommended that the features be analyzed to see if this suspicion might be verified. It was also noted that wood-working was probably carried out at area B. By contrast, area D did not contain artifacts with residues indicating wood-working, and the artifacts containing animal residues were not the type usually associated with hide processing (i.e., scrapers) Rather, the artifacts from this area were those more normally associated with flesh cutting. Thus, this area may have been a fish or mammal processing site for the purposes of food consumption or storage.

REFERENCES CITED IN APPENDIX 4

Broderick, M.
    1979    Ascending paper chromatographic analysis archaeology. In: Lithic Micro-Wear Analysis, B. Hayden (ed.), pp. 375–83. New York: Academic Press.

    n.d.    Blood, fat, resin, and starch from stone tools. Paper presented at the Annual Meeting of the Canadian Archaeological Association, 1980, Saskatoon.

Bruier, F. L.
    1976    New clues to stone tool function: Plant and animal residues. American Antiquity 41(4):478–84.

Esau, K.
    1953    Plant Anatomy. New York: John Wiley and Sons.

Feigl, F.
    1966    Spot Tests in Organic Analysis. Amsterdam: Elseuir Publishing Company.

Frison, G. C.
    1968    A functional analysis of chipped stone tools. American Antiquity 33:149–55.

Hawk, P. B., B. L. Oser, and W. H. Summerson
    1947    Physiological Chemistry. Toronto: The Blackiston Company.

Hayden, B.
    1979    Lithic Use-Wear Analysis. New York: Academic Press.

Hester, T. R., D. Gilbow, and A. B. Albe
    1973    A functional analysis of the Clear Forks artifacts from the Rio Grande Plain, Texas. American Antiquity 39:90–96.

Johansen, D. A.
    1940    Plant Microtechnique. New York: McGraw-Hill.

Keeley, L. H.
    1974    Technique and methodology in microwear studies: A critical review. World Archaeology 5:323–26.
    1980    Experimental determination of stone tool uses: A microwear analysis. Chicago: University of Chicago Press.

Morrison, R. T. and R. N. Boy
    1967    Organic Chemistry. Boston: Allyn and Bacon Inc.

Nance, J. D.
    1970    Lithic analysis: Implications for the prehistory of Central California. University of California, Department of Anthropology, Archaeology Survey Annual Report 12:62–103.

    1971    Functional interpretations from microscopic analysis. American Antiquity 36: 361–66.

Odell, G. C.
  1980 Toward a more behavioral approach to archaeological lithic concentrations. American Antiquity 45(3):404–31.

Parry, E. J.
  1925 Resins. In: Allen's Commercial Organic Analysis 4, S. S. Sadtler et al. (eds.). Philadelphia: P. Blackiston's Son and Co. Ltd.

Pearse, A. G. E.
  1960 Histochemistry: Theoretical and Applied. London: Churchill.

Semenov, J. A.
  1964 Prehistoric Technology. London: Cory, Adams, and MacKay.

Shafer, H. J., and R. G. Holloway
  1979 Organic residue analysis in determining stone tool function. In: Lithic Use-Wear Analysis, B. Hayden (ed.). New York: Academic Press.

Singer, C. A., and R. Gibson
  1970 The Medea Creek Village site: A functional lithic analysis. University of California, Los Angeles Department of Anthropology. Archaeology Survey Annual Report 12:188–203.

Wilmsen, E. N.
  1970 Lithic analysis and cultural inference: A Paleo-Indian case. University of Arizona Anthropological Papers 16.

# UMMA Backlist

Four series of publications are available from the Publications Office of the University of Michigan Museum of Anthropology. The Occasional Contributions, published from 1932 through 1956, and the Anthropological Papers, begun in 1949, are two series of short monographs, while the Memoirs, first published in 1970, are longer, more detailed studies. The fourth series, Technical Reports, begun in 1971, are brief, highly technical discussions of recent advances in several areas of anthropological study. New subseries will be added to the Technical Reports from time to time. Contributions to all of the series are prepared by staff members, associates, and friends of the Museum and include descriptions of museum collections and field work, results of research in various anthropological fields, and discussions of field and museum techniques.

John D. Speth, Director
Museum of Anthropology

The books below may be ordered from the Museum of Anthropology, 4009 Museums, University of Michigan, Ann Arbor, MI 48109. Libraries and members of the Michigan Archaeological Society receive a 20% discount. Checks must be in U.S. funds drawn on a U.S. bank. Please include $2 postage for all orders less than $10. Prepayment is required.

## Occasional Contributions

6. The Younge Site: An Archaeological Record from Michigan, by Emerson F. Greenman. 1937. Reprinted 1967. Pages 172, 33 plates, 9 figures, 10 maps. Price $3.00.
15. Araucanian Culture in Transition, by Mischa Titiev. 1951. Pages 164, 17 plates, 9 figures, 2 maps. Price $2.50.

## Anthropological Papers

13. The Puerto Rican Population: A Study of Human Biology, by Frederick P. Thieme. 1959. Pages 156, 4 figures, 2 maps. Price $2.50.
14. Tell Toqaan: A Syrian Village, by Louise E. Sweet. 1960. Pages 280, 54 figures. Price $2.50.
31. A Prehistoric Sequence in the Middle Pecos Valley, New Mexico, by Arthur J. Jelinek. 1967. Pages 190, 21 figures, 16 plates, Price $3.00.
34. The Prehistory of the Burnt Bluff Area, edited by James E. Fitting. 1968. Pages 140, 47 figures. Price $3.00.
39. Rules of Descent: Studies in the Sociology of Parentage, by Guy E. Swanson. 1969. Pages 108. 4 figures, 7 tables. Price $2.00.
40. Early Puebloan Occupations at Tesuque By-Pass and the Upper Rio Grande Valley, by Charles H. McNutt. 1969. Pages 140, 13 figures, 11 plates. Price $3.00.
41. The Archaeology of Summer Island: Changing Settlement Systems in Northern Lake Michigan, by David S. Brose. 1970. Pages 236, 31 tables, 17 figures, 35 plates. Price $3.00.
42. The Occupations of Migrants in Ghana, by Polly Hill. 1970. Pages 84, 11 tables. Price $2.00.
43. Prehistoric Biological Relationships in the Great Lakes Region, by Richard Guy Wilkinson. 1971. Pages 168, 40 tables, 33 figures, 2 plates. Price $3.50.

44. Property Control and Social Strategies: Settlers on a Middle Eastern Plain, by Barbara C. Aswad. 1971. Pages 180, 16 tables, 33 figures, 2 plates. Price $3.50.
48. The Wardell Buffalo Trap 48 SU 301: Communal Procurement in the Upper Green River Basin, Wyoming, by George C. Frison. 1973. Pages 111, 29 figures, 6 tables, 14 plates. Price $3.00.
50. Faction and Conversion in a Plural Society: Religious Alignments in the Hindu Kush, by Robert Leroy Canfield. 1973. Pages 142, 11 figures, 4 tables, 1 appendix. Pricce $3.00.
55. The Ait Ndhir of Morocco: A Study of the Social Transformation of a Berber Tribe, by Amal Rassam Vinogradov. 1974. Pages 128, 11 figures, 13 plates. Price $4.00.
59. An Analysis of Effigy Mound Complexes in Wisconsin, by William M. Hurley. 1975. Pages 466, 63 figures, 48 tables, 45 plates. Price $8.00.
60. Yerbas de la gente: A Study of Hispano-American Medicinal Plants, by Karen Cowan Ford. 1975. Pages 438, 1 figures. Price $5.00.
62. The Demography of the Semai Senoi, by Alan G. Fix. 1977. Pages 123, 17 figures, 38 tables. Price $5.00.
63. Economic and Social Organization of a Complex Chiefdom: The Halelea District, Kauai, Hawaii, by Timothy Earle. 1978. Pages 205, 27 figure, 7 tables, 6 plates. Price $6.00.
64. Wāsita in a Lebanese Context: Social Exchange Among Villagers and Outsiders, by Frederick Charles Huxley. 1978. Pages 174, 6 figures, 47 tables, 5 plates. Price $6.00.
65. Meadowood Phase Settlement Patterns in the Niagara Frontier Region of Western New York State, by Joseph E. Granger, Jr. 1978. Pages 403, 73 figures, 113 tables, 35 plates. Price $8.00.
66. The Snodgrass Site of the Powers Phase of Southeast Missouri, by James E. Price and James B. Griffin. 1979. Pages 189, 80 figures, 2 tables, 17 plates. Price $6.00.
67. The Nature and Status of Ethnobotany, edited by Richard I. Ford. 1978. Pages 428, 33 figures, 28 tables, 24 plates. Price $10.00.
68. The Biological and Social Analyses of a Mississippian Cemetery from Southeast Missouri: The Turner Site, 23BU21A, by Thomas K. Black III. 1979. Pages 170, 7 figures, 69 tables, 10 plates. Price $6.00.
69. The Ait Ayash of the High Molouuya Plain: Rural Social Organization in Morocco, by John Chiapuris. 1980. Pages 186, 15 figures 9 maps, 12 plates. Price $6.00.
70. An Early Woodland Community at the Schultz Site 20SA2 in the Saginaw Valley and the Nature of Early Woodland Adaptation in the Great Lakes Region, by Doreen Ozker. 1982. Pages 273, 27 tables, 33 figures, 15 plates. Price $10.00.
71. Persian Diary, 1939–1941, by Walter N. Koelz. 1983. Pages 227, 2 maps, 68 photos. Price $10.00.
72. Lulu Linear Punctated: Essays in Honor of George Irving Quimby, edited by Robert C. Dunnell and Donald K. Grayson. 1983. Pages 354, 39 figures, 19 plates, 20 tables. Price $12.00.
73. Paleoethnobotany of the Kameda Peninsula Jomon, by Gary W. Crawford. 1983. Pages 200, 27 figures, 12 tables, 23 plates. Price 48.00.
74. The Archaeology of the Sierra Blanca Region of Southeastern New Mexico, by Jane Holden Kelley. 1983. Pages 527, 85 figures, 10 maps, 41 tables, 87 plates. Price $15.00.
75. Prehistoric Food Production in North America, edited by Richard I. Ford. 1985. Pages 411, 39 figures, 22 tables. Price $15.00.
76. Primitive Polluters: Semang Impact on the Malaysian Tropical Rain Forest Ecosystem, by A. Terry Rambo. 1985. Pages 104, 5 figures, 5 tables, 16 plates. Price $8.00.
77. Jumano and Patarabueye: Relations at La Junta de los Rios, by J. Charles Kelley. 1986. Pages 180, 14 figures, 9 plates. Price $10.00.

**Memoirs**

2. The Burial Complexes of the Knight and Norton Mounds in Illinois and Michigan, by James B. Griffin, Richard E. Flanders and Paul F. Titterington. 1970. Pages 216, 177 plates. Price $7.00.
3. Prehistoric Settlement Patterns in the Texcoco Region, Mexico, by Jeffrey R. Parsons. 1971. Pages 447, 8 tables, 14 maps, 88 figures, 57 plates. Price $8.00.
4. The Schultz Site at Green Point: A Stratified Occupation Area in the Saginaw Valley of Michigan, edited by James E. Fitting. 1972. Pages 317, 84 figures, 70 tables, 2 appendixes. Price $8.00.
7. Formative Mesoamerican Exchange Networks with Special Reference to the Valley of Oaxaca, by Jane w. Pires-Ferreira. Prehistory and Human Ecology of the Valley of Oaxaca, Vol. 3. Pages 111, 44 figures, 27 tables, 4 plates. Price $6.00.
8. Fábrica San José and Middle Formative Society in the Valley of Oaxaca, by Robert D. Drennan. Prehistory and Human Ecology of the Valley of Oaxaca, Vol. 4. 1975. Pages 300, 10 tables, 2 maps, 75 figures, 29 plates. Price $8.00.
9. Studies in the Archaeological History of the Deh Luran Plain, by Frank Hole. 1977. Pages 369, 94 tables, 119 illustrations, 55 plates. $10.00.
10. Part 1. The Vegetational History of the Oaxaca Valley, by C. Earle Smith, Jr. Pages 39, 1 table, 2 maps, 10 plates. Part 2. Zapotec Plant Knowledge: Classification, Uses, and Communication About Plants in Mitla, Oaxaca, Mexico, by Ellen Messer. Pages 149, 29 figures, 1 map, 10 plates. Prehistory and Human Ecoloy of the Valley of Oaxaca, Vol. 5. 1978. Price $8.00.
11. An Archaeological Survey of the Keban Reservoir Area of East-Central Turkey, by Robert E. Whallon. 1979. Pages 309, 211 figures, 20 tables, 2 plates. Price $10.00.
12. Excavations at Santo Domingo Tomaltepec: Evolution of a Formative Community in the Valley of Oaxaca, Mexico, by Michael E. Whalen. Prehistory and Human Ecology of the Valley of Oaxaca, Vol. 6. 1981. Pages 225, 38 tables, 58 figures, 73 plates. Price $13.00.
13. An Early Town on the Deh Luran Plain: Excavations at Tepe Farukhabad, edited by Henry T. Wright. 1981. Pages 462, 99 figures, 96 tables, 21 plates. Price $15.00.
14. Prehispanic Settlement Patterns in the Southern Valley of Mexico: The Chalco-Xochimilco Region, by Jeffrey R. Parsons, Elizabeth Brumfiel, Mary H. Parsons, and David J. Wilson. 1982. Pages 504, 128 figures, 115 tables, 40 maps, 31 plates. Price $16.00.
15. Monte Albán's Hinterland, Part 1: The Prehispanic Settlement Patterns of the Central and Southern Parts of the Valley of Oaxaca, Mexico, by Richard E. Blanton, Stephen Kowalewski, Gary Feinman, and Jill Appel. Prehistory and Human Ecology of the Valley of Oaxaca, Vol. 7. 1982. Pages 506, 43 tables, 139 figures. Price $20.00.
16. A Fuego y Sangre: Early Zapotec Imperialism in the Cuicatlán Cañada, Oaxaca, by Elsa M. Redmond. Studies in Latin American Ethnohistory and Archaeology, Vol 1. 1983. Pages 216, 75 figures, 46 tables, 42 plates. Price $15.00.
17. Irrigation and the Cuicatec Ecosystem: A Study of Agriculture and Civilization in North Central Oaxaca, by Joseph W. Hopkins, III. Studies in Latin American Ethnohistory and Archaeology, Vol. 2. 1984. Pages 148, 13 figures, 3 tables, 16 plates. Price $15.00.
18. Aztec City-States, by Mary G. Hodge. Studies in Latin American Ethnohistory and Archaeology, Vol. 3. 1984. Pages 166, 64 figures, 30 tables. Price $15.00.
19. Early Neolithic Settlement and Society at Olszanica, by Sarunas Milisauskas. 1986. Pages 319, 160 figures, 153 tables, 51 plates. Price $20.00.
20. Chipped Stone Tools in Formative Oaxaca, Mexico: Their Procurement, Production and Use, by William J. Parry. Prehistory and Human Ecology of the Valley of Oaxaca, Vol. 8. 1987. Pages 178, 42 tables, 52 figures, 20 plates. Price $18.00.
21. Conflicts Over Coca Fields in XVIth-Century Perú, by María Rostworowski de Diez Canseco. Studies in Latin American Ethnohistory and Archaeology, Vol. 4. 1988. Pages 314, 21 figures, 2 tables. Price $19.50.

**Technical Reports**

2. LONGTERM and PEAKSCAN: Neutron Activation Analysis Computer Programs, by Thomas Meyers and Mark Denies. Contributions in Computer Applications to Archaeology, No. 2. 1972. Pages 76, 43 pages computer output, 2 figures. Price $1.00.
3. Data on the Abnormal Hemoglobins and Glucose-6-Phosphate Dehydrogenase Deficiency in Human Populations, by Frank B. Livingstone. Contributions in Human Biology, No. 1. 1973. Pages 289. Price $2.50.
4. An Arachaeological Investigation on the Loboi Plain, Baringo District, Kenya, by William R. Farrand, Richard W. Redding, Milford H. Wolpolff, and Henry T. Wright. Research Reports in Arcaeology, No. 1. 1976. Pages 59, 10 figures. Price $3.50.
5. Digging for Gold: Papers on Archaeology for Profit, edited by William K. Macdonald. Research Reports in Archaeology, No. 2. 1976. Pages 86. Price $3.50.
6. An Investigation of Ethnographic and Archaeological Specimens of Mescalbeans (*Sophora seconiflora*) in American Museums, by William L. Merrill. Research Reports in Ethnobotany, No. 1. 1977. Pages 167, 3 figures, 3 tables, 25 plates. Price $5.00.
7. Excavations at Quachilco: A Report on the 1977 Season of the Palo Blanco Project, by Robert D. Drennan. Research Reports in Archaeology, No. 3. Pages 81, 18 figures. Price $4.00.
10. Archaeological Investigations in Northeastern Xuzestan, 1976, edited by Henry T. Wright. Research Reports in Archaeology, No. 5. 1979. Pages 140, 52 figures, 20 tables. Price $6.00.
11. Prehistoric Social, Political, and Economic Development in the Area of the Tehuacan Valley: Some Results of the Palo Blanco Project, edited by Robert D. Drennan. Research Reports in Archaeology, No. 6. 1979. Pages 260, 46 figures, 26 tables. Price $6.50.
12. Late Prehistoric Bison Procurement in Southeastern New Mexico: The 1978 Season at the Garnsey Site, by John D. Speth and William J. Parry. Research Reports in Archaeology, No. 7. 1980. Pages 384, 39 figures, 32 tables, 34 plates. Price $9.00.
14. Archaeological Settlement Pattern Data from the Chalco, Xochimilco, Ixtapalapa, Texcoco and Zumpango Regions, Mexico, by Jeffrey R. Parson, Keith W. Kintigh, and Susan Gregg. Research Reports in Archaeology, No. 9. Pages 222. Price $8.00.
15. The Garnsey Spring Campsite: Late Prehistoric Occupation in Southeastern New MExico, by William J. Parry and John D. Speth. Research Reports in Archaeology, No. 10. Pages 228, 24 figures, 27 tables, 24 photos. Price $8.00.
16. Regional Archaeology in the Valle de la Plata, Colombia: A Preliminary Report on the 1984 Season of the Proyecto Arqueológico Valle de la Plata, edited by Robert D. Drennan. Research Reports in Archaeology, No. 11. 1985. Pages 195 (including complete Spanish translation), 43 figures, 16 tables. Price $8.00.
17. Zooarchaeology of Six Prehistoric Sites in the Sierra Blanca Region, New Mexico, by Jonathan C. Driver. Research Reports in Archaeology, No. 12. 1985. Pages 103, 29 tables, 8 figures, 1 appendix. Price $5.00.
18. The Henderson Site Burials: Glimpses of a Late Prehistoric Population in the Pecos Valley, by Thomas R. Rocek and John D. Speth. Research Reports in Archaeology, No. 13. 1986. Pages 348, 118 figures, 63 tables. Price $13.00.
19. Medicinal Plants of Native America, by Daniel E. Moerman. 1987. Pages 912 (in 2 vols.). Price $30.00.
20. Late Intermediate Occupation at Cerro Azul, Peru, by Joyce Marcus. 1987. Pages 112, 70 figures. Price $8.00.
21. The Inscriptions of Calakmul: Royal Marriage at a Maya City in Campeche, Mexico, by Joyce Marcus. 1987. Pages 205, 65 figures, 7 tables. Price $8.00.

**Special Publications**

The Williams Collection of Far Eastern Ceramics, Chinese, Siamese, and Annamese Ceramic Wares Selected from the Collection of Justice and Mrs. G. Mennen Williams in the University of Michigan Museum of Anthropology, by Kamer Aga-Oglu. 1972. Pages 73, 85 black and white photographs. Price $4.00.

The Williams Collection of Far Eastern Ceramics—Tonnancour Section, by Kamer Aga-Oglu. 1975. Pages 185, 183 black and white photographs, 18 color photographs. Price $8.00.